Enneagram Self-Discovery

Understand Personality Types to Enhance
Your Spiritual Growth & Build Healthy
Relationships

Elliot Hudson & Richard Matthews

Table of Contents

Free Mini Guide Reveals: How to **Banish Your Enneagram Type's Biggest Fear** in a Matter of Seconds!

As a way of saying thank you for your purchase, I'm offering a **FREE guide** that's *exclusive* the readers of this book.

The enneagram can be a very helpful tool when it comes to understanding your insecurities, fears, and roadblocks. But what steps should you take to overcome these struggles? This mini guide will take you to the roots of your behaviors and explain why you have the fears and temptations you do, and what steps you can take to annihilate them instantly!

Having a core fear is an unavoidable part of life, but it's what we do with this fear that makes the difference between bondage and abundant life!

An amazing fearless life is only seconds away!

Just go to: www.**FearlessCode.SelfRenewal.org** to get this free guide now!

Introduction

Perhaps the question most integral to the human experience is the question of identity. *Who am I?* is something we find ourselves asking over and over again. This is a question that both excites and terrifies. It opens up endless possibilities and imposes terrible restrictions. In the constant search for our own true selves, we often paradoxically end up burying our true identities deep within ourselves to shield ourselves from rejection and shame.

We build our identities around external social markers, around what we've done and what we have, instead of building our identities around who we really are. The tighter we cling to those external social markers, the more difficult it becomes to face and find our true selves. The more we allow external labels to define us, the more invested we become in protecting our social identities. In this self-defensive state, it's often our true selves we end up turning away for the sake of

3

social preservation.

According to Henri Nouwen, a philosopher, and theologian, there are three lies that most of us construct our identities around (Heuertz, 2017):

1) I am what I have.
2) I am what I do.
3) I am what others say or think about me.

These lies bring us comfort and sanctuary in the short term, but they are ultimately based not on truth, but on fear. If I believe I am what I have, then if I lose what I have, who am I? If I believe I am what I do, if I choose (or am forced) to do something different, who am I? If I believe I am only the sum of my social projections, then I am always at the mercy of others, with no agency over my own being. These lies bind us tighter and tighter to our own fears and insecurities until we find ourselves living in a perpetual state of spiritual crisis.

This is where the Enneagram comes in. The Enneagram is a self-discovery tool with roots in ancient spiritualities that has been augmented

4

with modern psychology. It's a guide to help us find our true personalities and shed the false social identities that we've built up around our true selves like a spiritual exoskeleton. Unlike astrology, the Enneagram won't ask you to consult the position of the sun and moon at the time of your birth. Nor is there a clinical examination for you to sit through like the Myers-Briggs Personality Test. Think of the Enneagram as somewhere in between these two approaches. It uses both ancient intuition and modern intellect to awaken us to our true fears, desires, gifts, and shortcomings.

The origins of the Enneagram are unclear. The nine-pointed star appears in spiritual texts in Europe and the Middle East far back into the medieval period. However, the ways that medieval monks, scholars, and philosophers used it seem to indicate an oral tradition that potentially extends much further back before its first appearance in text. Some sources trace the Enneagram back to the Christian monk Evagrius, the same monk who developed the theory of the Seven Deadly Sins, or the Franciscan monk Ramon Lull (Rohr, 2001). However, others have traced it back to the fourth century, where spiritual leaders in the Arabian peninsula used it for spiritual guidance and counselling. Still others can trace the Enneagram (or at least elements of it) back to the early teachings of Sufism or Judaism. Some even claim that the Enneagram's supposedly "ancient" origins are really the invention of occultists in Britain and the Americas in the early 1900s.

Regardless of its ancient (or not so ancient) past, in the 1970s a Chilean psychologist named Oscar Ichazo happened upon a version of the Enneagram that intrigued him. Together with his pupil Claudio Naranjo, he is responsible for bringing knowledge of modern psychology to the ancient tool and fine-tuning its system to what it is today. His pupil Naranjo brought this new personality system to the United States, where it caught the attention of Robert Ochs, a priest and instructor at Loyola University. Ochs brought the Enneagram back to Loyola, where it impressed (and has continued to impress) a number of

Christian scholars and theologians, many of whom have written definitive works on the Enneagram (Cron, 2016).

The Enneagram, then, does not belong to any one religion. It's not Christian, Sufi, or Jewish. It's not a clinically developed test, but neither is it esoteric mysticism. It's a system that comes from many different influences and has been built on the wisdom of multiple cultures, disciplines, and individual scholars who continue to refine and expand upon this unique spiritual approach to self-actualization. Thus, the Enneagram has attracted people from all different religious and scientific backgrounds, and is perhaps one of the few spiritual resources we have in the modern world that is far more uniting than it is polarizing.

The word "Enneagram" is Greek in origin, from the words "ennea," meaning nine, and "gram," meaning a written figure or symbol. This is in reference to the nine-pointed star that is used to represent the Enneagram's nine different personality types. This star is typically contained within a circle, with the nine personality points each set forty degrees from each other. The types are numbered clockwise from one to nine, with nine appearing at 12 o'clock. Each of the nine types outlines a distinct perceptual filter, or a unique way through which you have come to relate to the world. These nine distinct perceptions come with a supporting set of emotional energies, all of which combine to form our basic fears, motivations, desires, and personality traits. Each type is founded upon a fundamental need, something that individuals of that type believe is essential for their survival, satisfaction, and security. Each type also comes with a "root sin," or an essential darkness that individuals of that personality type must be constantly vigilant against. Learning your type will teach you what is most important to you, what your values are, where you direct most of your energy, and how to understand your own behavior.

Remember that the Enneagram is not useful as a label. Rather, it should be approached as a self-awakening tool, a way for you to become fully opened to your unique perceptions of the world. Rather than putting you into a box or stereotype, the Enneagram personality types are archetypes against which you can evaluate your own motivations, fears, and behaviors, and take more agency over your own spiritual well-being.

The basis of the Enneagram is not to add, but to dismantle. When you begin working with the Enneagram, you will not be adding anything new to bolster your ego or decorate your personality. Instead, you will be going deeply within. Working with the Enneagram requires a deep level of introspection. By diving deeply within yourself, you'll be better able to understand how you relate to others, and in turn, you'll have a much clearer vision of how the world relates to you. Rather than asking you to believe something new about yourself, the Enneagram will ask you to "unbelieve" the lies you've been telling yourself.

It's very easy to feel lost or uncertain about our identities, especially in the digital age. All day long we are bombarded with ideas and images that enforce the three lies summarized by Nouwen. Advertisements are constantly telling us what we should have. Politicians, educators, and even our own families use the access they have with modern technology to tell us what we should be doing. And social media is constantly asking us to evaluate what other people think of us.

In the midst of all this noise, it has become ever more important to find a way to retreat within ourselves. The Enneagram can help us to find the stillness and silence that we need to return to our true selves when the distractions of modern life become too overwhelming. When we feel that we have lost ourselves, the Enneagram is our spiritual GPS to help us find our way back to who we really are.

This book will give you the tools you need to discover your own Enneagram type, and will provide you with a basic guide to the fears, motivations, strengths, weaknesses, and characteristics typically displayed by individuals of the same type. This book will also encourage you to go back to your formative experiences as a child, as each personality type is essentially formed as a defense mechanism to protect ourselves from threats we experienced during our formative years (Daniels, 2009). In psychological terms, the "root sin" of each type is a defense mechanism that has become pathologized. In order to work through your root sin, you will need to first discover the initial threats that made your defenses necessary before you can begin to dismantle them.

This book will speak to you on a deep and truthful level. It will confirm things you are already aware of and articulate what you've always known but have never vocalized before. These moments will be revelatory, powerful, and affirming, and are an important part of the process as you begin to work with the Enneagram. On the other hand, this book will also make you uncomfortable. Becoming self-aware is often painful or uncomfortable. You may be asked to look at yourself in a new or uncomfortable way. The new clarity which enables you to embrace your gifts will also give you an unobstructed view of your shortcomings. But part of working with the Enneagram is working through these feelings of shame or discomfort. Challenging our constructed identities is the only way we can find the truth and come to know who we really are. Self-discovery is not only about embracing the things we like about ourselves, but learning to love, forgive, and transform the things about ourselves that we aren't proud of.

As you confront these uncomfortable moments, remember that learning your type is only the beginning. This book will provide you with exercises, meditations, and guides to help you work with your unique fears and challenges and embrace your true strengths and gifts, but you will be learning the lessons of the Enneagram long after you put this book down. Again, think of the Enneagram as a GPS for the soul, a guiding voice to help you find your way to where you want to go.

The first step to using the Enneagram, of course, is learning your type. This book will provide you with the tools you need to discover your type, as well as a thorough introduction into the various characteristics of that type. Remember that everyone's personalities and experiences are unique, and we don't always fit neatly into one type or another. To acknowledge this, this book will also outline some common mis-typings to help put you back on track if you feel like the type you've been given doesn't quite fit.

The next step is to learn your wing number. If you like astrology, think of your type number as your sun, and your wing number as your ascendant. If you don't like astrology, your type number is the core of your personality, but your wing is a complementary influence that can affect your behaviors and characteristics. For example, a Type 4 with a Wing 3 will be outgoing and extroverted, while a Type 4 with a Wing 5 will be more introverted and withdrawing. Working with your wing number will give you a more accurate view of your type number, and is most helpful in understanding your social responses, especially in close or intimate relationships.

You will also learn your stress number. Your type number will tell you what kinds of situations stress you out, but your stress number will tell you what kinds of behaviors you adopt in response to that stress. Do you ever feel like you aren't yourself when you're under a lot of pressure? Well, you're not exactly wrong. Stress is a powerful physical and emotional force, and it does "change our personalities" when it presents in extreme cases. This is both natural and normal. This emotional stress response is the way your soul protects itself. Learning your stress number will help you understand who you become when you're under stress, and embrace that person as just another facet of your unique personality.

Finally, you will learn your security number. Just as you draw from another type when you are feeling stressed, you also draw from another number when you are feeling most secure. Remember, every type number is founded on an essential spiritual "need." So when that need is filled, our personalities expand, and we uncover new perspectives. Learning your security number will help you to embrace that new perspective, and so will allow you to embrace the changes that come with security and fulfillment, rather than withdrawing from those changes in fear for your "identity."

The nine personality types are also divided into different "stances." Your type's stance is the underlying attitude that governs all of your type's behavioral characteristics. What these Stances mean for each individual type will make more sense after reading through the descriptions of each type, but here I will start you off with a general outline of the different stances and what they mean (Stabile, 2018):

- **Aggressive (3, 7, 8):** These numbers enjoy being in control. They are fully independent and strong-willed, sometimes to a fault. They are constantly looking forward to the future.
- **Dependent (1, 2, 6):** These numbers place a high value on their relationships with others, sometimes even above their own

individual needs. They are the personalities most able to remain fully mindful of the present without becoming tangled in guilts from the past or anxieties about the future.

- **Withdrawing (4, 5, 9):** These numbers tend to be very shy and introverted. These people often look back to the past for answers to problems in the present.

In general, numbers of the same stance tend to get along best with each other. They have similar orientations, worldviews, and fears. However, if your wing number is in a different stance from your type number, that will often help you to get along with numbers in both stances, and means that you sometimes take on the behavioral characteristics of your wing stance. If your wing and type number are in the same stance, on the other hand, it tends to magnify the behaviors associated with that stance group, and can make it harder for you to relate to numbers in the other two stances.

At this point, you are probably eager to begin your journey, but before you continue on, one more word of advice. When you learn your type number, it will be tempting to skip straight to that part and read no more. But try to resist this temptation. Of course, your type will be the type you want to focus on and work with the most closely. But understanding all of the numbers will give you a better understanding of the other personality types that are manifesting themselves all around you. The better you understand each number, the better you will begin to understand the people around you, and even begin recognizing personality types in your family, partners, and friends.

And with that, let's begin!

The Basics

What is the Enneagram?

Pronounced ANY-a-gram, the system of the Enneagram is based on nine fundamental personality types. These types are based on a mix of ancient mysticism and modern psychological understandings of how personality is formed and how it's related to behavior. Is it a religion? No, but religious people have written about it and successfully incorporated it into Christian, Jewish, Sufi, and other religious practices. Is it a science? Again, not really, but psychologists, therapists, and others interested in personal growth and wellness have also successfully incorporated it into their daily lives and even clinical practices. If you like mystic personality tools like astrology, then the Enneagram provides you with a similar spiritual lens, but one that is more concerned with the conditions of your upbringing than with the position of the planets at your time of birth. If you like clinical personality tests like Myers-Briggs, then the Enneagram provides you with a similar psychologically sound tool for personal growth, but one that is just as concerned with your inner fears and desires as it is with your behaviors and motivations. In short, this is a system that is open to people of all spiritual, cultural, and academic backgrounds, and one that has been enhanced, taught, and influenced by voices from humans of all walks of life.

Discovering your type is not meant to tell you who you are. Instead, it's meant to offer you objective insight into your own inner workings. The nine types all arise in early childhood as defense mechanisms against external threats. They are a perceptual lens that we share with others who have encountered similar formative experiences. The identities that are presented to you by the Enneagram are not based in social identities like class, gender, or sexuality. In fact, what you will uncover when you begin using the Enneagram is likely to challenge the identities and roles that you've constructed for yourself around these external social labels. This isn't to say that social labels aren't important or don't have a very real impact on the ways in which we relate to the world. But what the Enneagram will do is allow you to construct your social identities based on your true self, rather than doing the opposite.

The Enneagram diagram is a nine-pointed star contained within a circle. The nine points each correspond to one of the nine personality types, moving clockwise from one to nine, with nine positioned at 12 o'clock. The connecting lines of the star are actually arrows that point in two directions: the direction of security and the direction of stress. Later in this book you will learn how to follow those directional arrows in order to discover your stress number and your security number, and learn the personality traits that you take on in situations of extreme stress and extreme security.

The nine types of the Enneagram can be briefly described as follows (Wagele, 1994):
- Type 1: The Perfectionist (realistic, conscientious, principled)

- Type 2: The Helper (warm, concerned, nurturing)
- Type 3: The Achiever (energetic, optimistic, self-assured)
- Type 4: The Individualist (sensitive, warm, perceptive)
- Type 5: The Investigator (intellectual, introverted, curious)
- Type 6: The Questioner (responsible, trustworthy, loyal)
- Type 7: The Enthusiast (energetic, lively, optimistic)
- Type 8: The Challenger (direct, self-reliant, self-confident)
- Type 9: The Peacemaker (receptive, good-natured, supportive)

These types can all be divided in two ways: according to stance and according to center. If you remember from the introduction, stance refers to attitude, and how these types relate to the world. Center refers to desires, and how these types relate to or define themselves. The sections dedicated to each type will explain their stance and center in detail, but I will put a quick overview of the centers here:

- **Heart (2, 3, 4)**: These types are interested in people, like to be seen in a good light, and have a strong need to express themselves.
- **Head (5, 6, 7)**: These types are very active, and rely on their own resources and guidance from authority figures to provide security.
- **Gut (8, 9, 1)**: These types are most concerned with the world as it appears in front of them, and react first and foremost according to their instincts.

Because these groupings have more to do with internal forces than external motivators, numbers with the same center don't necessarily relate well to each other. For example, 2s and 3s are both interested in people, but 2s want primarily to be nurturers and caretakers, while 3s want to be liked and taken care of. Your center is also influenced by your wing number, and that can change the way that you act upon your center desires. For example, a Type 4 with a Wing 5 will use their own resources to assert their unique personality, while a Type 4 with a Wing 3 will often assert their individuality by comparing themselves with others.

Before you begin the journey toward discovering your type, it's important to understand where the Enneagram came from and how these different types have been developed into the spiritual system in use today.

Where Does It Come From?

Christian theologians tend to trace the Enneagram back to three historical sources: Evagrius Ponticus, Ramon Lull, and Ignatius of Loyola. Whether or not the Enneagram truly begins with these three theologians, they are the first recorded people to use the Enneagram in a Christian context (Ahlberg, 2019).

Evagrius Ponticus was an early church leader in medieval Christianity. Most of his work was invested in moving away from the idea that spirituality is about cleansing the soul of sin and creating a Christian philosophy that was more concerned with spirituality as a way to become more connected with God. In addition to his work

23

as an early Christian theologian, he was also a philosopher, mystic, and scientist. His work as a scientist influenced his spiritual writings as well. He believed that spiritual awakening was connected to intellectual understanding. Much of his work (including his work with the Enneagram) combined theories from Pythagorean geometry and astronomy with spirituality, and he believed that using numbers in spiritual practice would create orderly rhythms of the spirit that reflected and complemented the orderly rhythms of the Earth and space. Much of his later work was more psychological in nature, and he became interested in discovering behaviors and feelings that stopped people from becoming their best selves. It's this work that would eventually lead to the theory of the Seven Deadly sins. Each of the Enneagram numbers has a corresponding "vice," and the idea that each personality has a root weakness can be traced back to Evagrius.

Ramon Lull was a 12th century Franciscan monk and theologian. He did a lot of work with the Enneagram diagram itself, and the idea that the points of the star can be followed as arrows pointing in two directions (one toward security and one toward stress) can be traced back to him. He was highly influenced by the work of Evagrius, and much of his work with the Enneagram was focused on how its energies can be used to counteract our inner weaknesses.

Ignatius of Loyola spent most of his life as a soldier, and only turned to theology in the second half of his life. In his mid-forties he founded a spiritual order that would eventually become the Jesuits. Perhaps influenced by his migratory life as a warrior, this society was founded on the mission to spread knowledge of Christianity to all corners of the globe. Ignatius began working with the Enneagram as a tool to help his followers understand and discover their spiritual missions. Less concerned with vices, he began using the Enneagram as a way to uncover inner passions and motivations. The idea that the nine types can be divided into the three centers of gut, head, and heart can be traced back to him.

However, the Enneagram's ancient roots run deeper and wider than medieval Christian mysticism. There are records of the Enneagram being used in Sufi mysticism before Evagrius started writing about it, and there's a great deal of evidence to suggest that it was introduced to Christian scholars via Sufi texts (Berghoef, 2017). In Europe, the scientific preoccupations of the Renaissance came into direct conflict with Christian church leaders, which led to a polarizing of religion and science. This polarization caused Christian dogma to become a lot more conservative, and much of the work of the medieval mystics was condemned or forgotten, including the Enneagram.

However, it continued to live on through Sufism, continuously used and expanded upon by Muslim thinkers and scholars until well into the 19th century. The Enneagram was not reintroduced to Europe until the early 19th century, when it started being used by a Russian occultist named G.I. Gurdjieff. He introduced the Enneagram to Russia as a tool for reading spiritual energies, and it became the basis for many of the spiritual dances and chants he taught to his followers. These dances were choreographed using the Enneagram as a way to physically connect with the movement of spiritual forces. He also used the Enneagram as a way for individual people to discover their "chief feature," or a defining personality trait that ultimately stopped them from accessing their inner selves. His work with the Enneagram to help students balance their emotional, mental, and physical wellness is the first documented incident of the Enneagram being used as a personality tool.

His work would later inspire Chilean psychologist Oscar Ichazo when he discovered the Enneagram in the 1950s. In the 1970s, he would eventually publish the basis of the tool that we now use as the modern Enneagram, a cohesive interweaving of occultism and modern psychology. He is the first person to develop the nine points of the Enneagram into distinct personality types, and assigned each of the nine types a defining emotional weakness and a defining strength.

Ichazo's student Claudio Naranjo did more work with the Enneagram in the late 1970s and early 1980s to expand upon the nine personality types. He created detailed profiles of each of the nine types, outlining their defining behaviors and characteristics, as well as their related pathologies. He assigned motivations, cognitive biases, and neurotic tendencies to each type. He also developed the first Enneagram test to help people discover their personality type.

Naranjo began teaching and publishing his work on the Enneagram in California. Local Jesuit missionaries who attended one of his lectures on the Enneagram were greatly inspired by it, and so it was subsequently reintroduced to Christian theology in the late 1980s.

Structure

The figure of the Enneagram is a nine-pointed star surrounded by a circle. The nine points of the star each correspond to one of the nine personality types, going clockwise from one to nine, with nine at 12 o'clock. The star features an inner triangle that connects types 3, 6, and 9. These three types are the most dynamic types in their center groups. The other six types are connected by the hexad, or the remaining six points of the star.

The nine personality types all come with their own distinct behaviors, personality traits, fears, desires, and motivations. No one is purely one type, but we all have a core or dominant personality. This core personality is "your" type, or the set of personality traits that you most fully embody in your own life.

A complete profile of each type will appear in the sections dedicated to that type. But to understand the basic foundations of the Enneagram, we need to understand the types according to their names and their most basic identifiers. Each type has a root "sin," or essential spiritual weakness (Sherrill, 2016). Each type has a "basic fear," or a situation that they pour most of their energies into avoiding, whatever the cost. Each type has a pathology, or essential psychological weakness.

Type 1 - The Perfectionist

Root Sin: Anger

Basic Fear: Anger

Pathology: Hypersensitivity

Type 2 - The Helper

Root Sin: Pride

Basic Fear: Interdependence

Pathology: Flattery

Type 3 - The Achiever

Root Sin: Deceit

Basic Fear: Failure

Pathology: Vanity

Type 4 - The Individualist

Root Sin: Envy

Basic Fear: Ordinariness

Pathology: Melancholy

Type 5 - The Investigator

Root Sin: Avarice

Basic Fear: Emptiness

Pathology: Emotional Stinginess

Type 6 - The Questioner

Root Sin: Fear

Basic Fear: Lawlessness

Pathology: Cowardice or Recklessness

Type 7 - The Enthusiast
    Root Sin: Gluttony
    Basic Fear: Pain
    Pathology: Scheming
Type 8 - The Challenger
    Root Sin: Lust
    Basic Fear: Weakness
    Pathology: Revenge
Type 9 - The Peacemaker
    Root Sin: Laziness
    Basic Fear: Conflict
    Pathology: Lethargy

All of the types can be divided into three "centers," or essential attitudes through which that type relates to the world. Within these centers, however, each type has a "tendency," or a primary way in which that type expresses the central attitude:

- **Heart Center (2, 3, 4):** Social Direction - Towards Others

    Type 2 - Over-expresses emotions
    Type 3 - Most out of touch with emotions
    Type 4 - Under-expresses emotions

31

- **Head Center (5, 6, 7):** Social Direction - Away from Others

  Type 5 - Over-expresses thoughts

  Type 6 - Most out of touch with thoughts

  Type 7 - Under-expresses thoughts
- **Gut Center (8, 9, 1):** Social Direction - Against Others

  Type 8 - Over-expresses instincts

  Type 9 - Most out of touch with instincts

  Type 1 - Under-expresses instincts

As you begin the journey to self-awareness, you will first discover your own personality type. You'll begin to work with the strengths and weaknesses, motivations, desires, fears, pathologies, and gifts that are associated with that type. You'll begin working with your type's center intelligence, and work to develop your type's typical expression of that intelligence.

However, using the Enneagram is more than taking a simple test. Discovering your type is only the beginning, and though working with your type alone will open you up to some startling revelations about yourself, there is more to the Enneagram than its underlying structure. In total, you will be working with four different type numbers by the end of the book. The defining traits of all four numbers are constantly in flux within your unique personality, surfacing at different times in your life and in response to different circumstances. At the very beginning, when you are still opening yourself up to the process of self-observation, it is important to keep in mind that no matter what your type may be, it does not define you by itself. The Enneagram's star is encased in a circle for a reason. No one type is functioning in isolation. All of the types are connected to each other in one way or another, forming multiple layers of connection that, as you uncover them, will help you to become more and more connected with your true self.

Once you've started working with your type number, the next step is to discover your wing number. Your wing will be one of the two numbers adjacent to your type number. For example, if you are a Type 4, then your wing will either be 3 or 5. Your wing acts as a behavioral supplement to the traits associated with your type, exerting a subtle, but noticeable, difference on your personality. So if you are a Type 4 Wing 3, you will be much more warm, sociable, and outgoing than a Type 4 Wing 5. Understanding the core components of your wing type will help you to understand how it interacts with the traits of your main type, and begin to awaken you to how your wing traits manifest in your personality.

After you've discovered your type and your wing, you'll go back to the Enneagram star itself. The connecting lines of the star can be followed as arrows that move in two different directions. One direction leads to stress, the other to security. You will learn how to read the diagram in both directions, and learn your stress number and your security number. Your stress number is the type whose traits you draw from when you are feeling extreme pressure or anxiety, and your security number is the type whose traits you begin to access when your basic desires are being met.

If you are feeling confused, overwhelmed, or lost, don't worry! You're still at the beginning of your journey. Now that you have an idea of the Enneagram's basic structures, you can begin to see the many ways it can be used as a tool for self-discovery and growth.

How It Helps Us

Sure, personality tools and tests can be interesting and fun, but how does the Enneagram help us on our journey to becoming better people?

The primary gift of the Enneagram is the many categories and connections it contains, both within individual types and across the star as a whole. While these categories and connections can seem complicated and overwhelming at first, as you start working with the Enneagram in earnest, you'll begin to see how these connections are intricately layered, one over the other, in a way that very smoothly and efficiently guides you toward your deepest and truest self.

The Enneagram gives us an objectively (and sometimes brutally) honest look at ourselves. The view of our own personality we get from the Enneagram is not colored by judgment, expectations, past histories, or future expectations. Thus, it's something that we can rely on in moments of delusion, uncertainty, or self-doubt. It's this impartial guide that allows us to shed the false fronts we have built up around our true selves in order to protect ourselves from rejection.

Each type comes with a basic desire and a basic fear. This is the true starting point for working with the Enneagram and uncovering our hidden selves. Desire and fear seem so basic when we first approach the Enneagram. If someone asked you what you want and what you're afraid of, you'd likely have a ready answer.

But the Enneagram shows us that often the things we are afraid of are not the things we think we are afraid of, and the things we think we want are often not the things that we crave deep in our hearts. Once you've been awakened to the basic desires of your type, you'll start to notice how those desires shape your actions, and before you realize it, you'll be well down the path of self-discovery.

Our bodies are often much more difficult to fool than our brains. When our actions and our desires don't seem to match up, we tend to wonder why we aren't able to get the things we want, and never question the validity of those supposed "wants" in the first place. Often, learning the basic desires of your type puts many of your past actions (even ones that you aren't proud of) into sudden clarity. Your brain can convince itself that it wants something, but when called to action, the body will usually act in accordance with your true desires.

The same is true for our fears. We think we know what our fears are, and when we can't conquer them, we blame ourselves for our supposed cowardice. But the Enneagram shows us that our inadequate responses to the things we think we fear are often perfectly adequate responses to protect from the things that we truly fear. Learning your true fears will finally allow you to liberate yourself from them.

Using the Enneagram begins a life-long path of self-observation. As you are empowered to look more and more honestly at yourself, you'll probably discover that a lot of your self-talk is fairly toxic. The myriad ways we deceive ourselves every day make us feel momentarily secure, but they build up overtime to spiritually devastating consequences. Though the path of self-discovery can be unpleasant to walk sometimes, the more awakened you become to your true self, the less likely you will be to fall prey to the destructive thought and behavior patterns that currently have you in their grasp. Self-discovery is self-liberation. The truth will truly set you free from the obstacles you've put in your own way, and allow you to take agency over your actions. The Enneagram will empower you to begin acting with intention, rather than living in a constant state of reaction and self-preservation.

We are often called upon to just "be ourselves," but this seems to be a directive that's much easier said than done. The reality is, it's actually quite difficult to be ourselves if we don't know who we are. Worse, we are bombarded all day long with external messages that seek to affix labels to us. This is especially true now in the age of social media and 24/7 global connection. While it's true that we humans are more connected to each other than we've ever been, it's possibly also true that we are more disconnected from ourselves than we've ever been (Heuertz, 2019).

The Enneagram is the step back from constant barrage of labels, media, advertisements, and social connections that are continuously telling you who you should be, what you should want, and what you should fear. It gives you resilience against those who would manipulate you, and gives you an anchor in the sea of messages we are all sailing in the 21st century. The Enneagram is not giving you still more labels to pin to yourself. Instead, it's going to ask you to start peeling off the labels that are already stuck fast to your identity.

In an increasingly polarized world, the Enneagram also offers us a bridge between religion and science, two disciplines that seem to be forever at odds with one another. It offers a reconciliation between the need for spiritual fulfillment and the need for evidence-based observation. Regardless of your type, working with the Enneagram will gradually help you to become more comfortable with academic disciplines and cultural traditions that in other contexts may have been alienating or even oppressing. The Enneagram gives us the rare opportunity to meet others on equal footing, without the weight of political oppression or social fears to drag us down.

Self-Observation

We are not our personality (Riso, 2000). Rather, our personality is a manifestation of who we are, the way that we bring the inner self out into the world to thrive and grow. At least, that's how it's supposed to work. But sometimes our inner self gets lost, and retreats back to live deep inside us. It's easy to get swept up in the tides of life, and before we know it, we're stranded on a spiritual desert island, with no idea how we got there or how to get back home to our true selves.

The Enneagram is a tool for self-observation. It gives a new angle or clarity with which we can look at our own personalities, and therefore come to a more lucid understanding of who we are and what motivates us. However, the practice of self-observation doesn't begin when you learn your Enneagram type number. It begins now. You don't need the Enneagram to practice self-observation, just as you don't need a GPS to find your way around a new city. But like the GPS, the Enneagram offers you a guide, and makes the process much more fruitful and informative.

Practicing self-observation is taking agency over your own growth and understanding the role you have to play in your own spiritual transformation. The Enneagram won't change you—you will change you, and you will use the wisdom of the Enneagram to help you enact that transformation. Therefore, self-observation is integral to using the Enneagram in a beneficial way. If you expect the Enneagram to give you the answers, you will find the limitations of your type ossifying, rather than transforming or growing. But if you are always mindfully using the Enneagram as a checkpoint or guiding light to show you the way forward, then you will truly be able to use this tool to its utmost spiritual benefits.

To begin the process of self-observation, start questioning yourself. Right now, before you've even learned your type, what would you say your strengths are? What are your weaknesses? What are your defenses and anxieties? How do you react to frustration and disappointment? What are your gifts and talents?

Self-observation isn't a test. There's no right or wrong answer to these questions, and no answer that you give is wrong or even misguided. If you take the time to write down your answers to these questions, you might be shocked to go back and see what you wrote after you've started working with the Enneagram and been awakened to some of the truths it has to offer you. This is okay. In fact, it's perfectly normal. What this exercise shows us is that self-observation is a discipline. It's not something that we have a natural inclination for.

It's something that we need to practice in order to be good at it, and it is something that we have to spend some time developing before we can do it well.

Beginning the process of self-observation is about testing how well you know yourself or how connected you are to your inner truths. Instead, the process of self-observation is about revealing your illusions. It's about identifying your perceptions of yourself, so that you can liberate yourself from those perceptions and begin to embody your true self more fully.

It is also very important that you bring no self-judgment to the act of self-observation. If you are not living in accordance with your true self, why? What's creating the block? What's causing you to flee? If you've acted in ways that you are ashamed of, aren't proud of, or that contradict the person you are striving to become, then instead of condemning or punishing yourself, you must ask yourself why? Learning what's causing you to become spiritually disconnected is the only way to grow through your defense mechanisms and cast them off when they are no longer needed.

Self-observation is paired with self-understanding. If we can start seeing ourselves with more clarity, we can begin to understand why we do what we do, think what we think, and feel what we feel. Self-observation begins now, before you've even started working with the Enneagram. If you start questioning your perceptions now, it will greater facilitate the self-understandings that come with the discovery of your type number, and set you firmly on the path to self-transformation.

The more you practice self-observation, the more you will start to recognize your unconscious tendencies. We all have them—small habits that we've done so many times we are no longer aware of it. Self-observation, however, will start to make you more aware. Once you begin to see your unconscious tendencies, you can take steps to change before those tendencies become toxic or self-sabotaging habits. Self-observation helps you to see harmful patterns in your thoughts and behavior. It will give you the presence, patience, and awareness you need to change those patterns so that you are no longer victim to the inevitable consequences of these harmful patterns when they manifest over and over in your behavior.

Attitudes and actions are the two primary ways in which we relate to the world, and therefore, our attitudes and actions always have effects on the world around us. Toxic attitudes and actions poison our environment, and cause us to feel more and more trapped by our relationships and life situations. Self-observation will allow us to see our attitudes and actions for what they are, and therefore help to mediate the effects they have on our lives.

Our Relationships with Others

The Enneagram is not only a useful tool for learning more about ourselves. As you begin using the Enneagram and working with the nine personality types, you'll begin to recognize certain traits and characteristics in the people around you. Just as the Enneagram gives us the courage we need to face ourselves, it also gives us the empathy we need to have full and fulfilling relationships with other people (Riso, 1996).

The insight we get into our own characters, paradoxically, helps us to better understand other people because it gives us more insight into how we interact with others. Our social identities are often built around who we want to be, rather than who we are, and so they can often blind us to the ways in which we come across to other people. If we are unable to see ourselves honestly, then it can become very difficult to understand why other people (especially people whom we care about) respond to us in the ways that they do. On the other hand, the more clarity we have when viewing ourselves, the more clarity we have when viewing our interactions with others.

The objectivity that the Enneagram gives you in regards to your personality will help you to adjust your behavior when you are interacting with others to more honestly communicate your feelings, thoughts, desires, and fears. It will help you to adjust your behavior to better project who you truly are, and actively work toward who you want to be. The Enneagram offers us a path of genuine growth and transcendence that is both natural and healthy for our unique needs, rather than a one-size-fits-all model of "healthy" and "unhealthy" relationship strategies.

Too often, when we are struggling in our relationships, we find ourselves in an either-or mindset. Either I sacrifice my needs for the sake of the other person, or I assert my own needs at the cost of the other person. The middle ground often seems impossible to reach. But in most cases, the either-or mindset is a problem of perception, rather than reality. You aren't sure how to advocate for your own needs because you aren't sure what your needs really are. So you end up denying yourself unnecessarily or hurting others for the sake of something that, ultimately, wasn't worth the pain and resulting damage to your relationship.

Our social identities are often built on lies that we tell ourselves in order to feel worthy, important, or lovable. But our perceptions of others are often built on lies, too. We look at people through the lens of who we want them to be or who we think they should be, rather than accepting them for who they really are. Just as the Enneagram will begin to challenge the lies you tell yourself about yourself, it will also start to challenge the lies you tell yourself about other people. As you begin to see the traits and characteristics of each type manifesting in the people around you, you will become more awake to the fact that all beings (not just you) are working toward a basic desire, and fighting to protect themselves from a basic fear. Behaviors that once would have offended, threatened, or insulted you will start to make more sense, and often provide you the insight you need to safely avoid unnecessary pain or conflict.

When you start seeing the world with the nine personality types in mind, you will start to see the ways in which we all fall prey to our own personality biases, and how best to respond to those biases without compromising your own needs (Palmer, 1996). Much of the suffering we experience in our personal relationships is the result of emotional blindness, a fundamental inability to see things from the other person's point of view. Even if you don't know the type of the person you're working with, simply being aware of the many different personalities beyond your own will give you the presence of mind you need to bring empathy and compassion into your dealings with others rather than reacting from a place of defensiveness or confusion.

Each of the nine types expresses love, affection, fear, frustration, joy, sorrow, and anger in different ways. Not only will you learn how your own type expresses these different emotions, but you will be awakened to the fact that not everyone understands those feelings in exactly the same way. For example, if you are a Type 8, you probably express your love and respect for others by being blunt, upfront, and brutally honest about what you want and how you feel, and you probably expect others to do the same. But when you start working with the Enneagram, you will begin to realize that when others fail to be as "honest" as you about their feelings, they aren't trying to hide or manipulate you. Instead, they simply have different ways to express their love and respect, and may even be interpreting your "honesty" and "forthrightness" as criticism and pushiness.

As you would probably assume, certain types get along with one another more easily than with others (Riso, 2003). Learning your type will also teach you which types you naturally connect with and relate to, and which types you can find it more difficult to accept. When you are out in the world, you will have more awareness of what kinds of attitudes and behaviors work in harmony with your own, and which are more likely to hurt or frustrate you.

Spirituality

The real beauty of the Enneagram is that it doesn't belong purely to the realm of psychology or religion. Instead, it neatly fuses both of them to create something far more rich than the cold observations of science and far more spiritually fulfilling than the dogmas of religion. The Enneagram, truly, is a tool for spiritual development. Our personalities aren't the entirety of who we are, but they can limit our ability to access our inner selves if we aren't aware of them.

By allowing us to understand better the landscape of our psychology, the Enneagram allows us to have a richer and healthier relationship with reality. It allows us to experience ourselves and the world around us for what they truly are, rather than through the filter of our fears and perceptions. This new clarity opens us up to the possibility of a fuller experience of life, and this, in essence, is what spirituality is.

While the Enneagram is far from the only spiritual tool out there, other self-observation disciplines like meditation or yoga can take a long time to develop and can be difficult to integrate into a contemporary lifestyle. While this doesn't mean that the pursuit of other spiritual paths aren't worth the effort, the dedication and discipline that they require can pose a barrier to achieving spiritual wellness. The Enneagram puts up no such barrier because the Enneagram itself is not a discipline. All it offers you is insight—it's up to you to put your new knowledge into action.

The Enneagram opens us up to both the obstacles and supports to spiritual fulfillment that are already inherent within our own hearts and minds. Its guidance toward more spiritual living is about illuminating the path that we're currently walking, rather than the path we should or could or will eventually walk. The Enneagram's many layers of understanding help us to unveil what it is we need right now, without overwhelming us with the possibility of what we might be doing or needing further on in our journey. Thus, working with the

Enneagram might give you the presence of mind you need to begin serious engagement with a self-observation discipline. It works seamlessly with other spiritual traditions and practices, and opens the way for you to develop a more fully-realized connection with spiritual disciplines that were previously closed to you.

Presence is a word that's easy to understand, but it's the true spiritual gift of the Enneagram. Presence is what keeps us rooted in reality, and is therefore the ultimate weapon against anxiety and anger. When we are fully aware of ourselves, we are able to speak and act with intention, and are able to interact with the world as it is, not as we imagine it to be.

It offers us a map toward the fulfillment of our deepest spiritual needs by naming with great detail and specificity exactly what aspects of our personality are currently limiting us, and how we can use those same aspects to grow to our full spiritual potential. All aspects of the nine personalities are indicators of spiritual capability, and with this in mind, we are able to see even our most self-destructive attitudes and behaviors with compassion and understanding. This is what opens the way for true healing. This is the door that must be unlocked before we can discover who it is we really are.

This all-encompassing view of personality is what makes the Enneagram more than just a psychological test. While a diagnosis from the DSM can give us insight into the way our minds work, it doesn't give us any guidance as to how to grow or transform ourselves into our more full and complete selves. Psychology is too often preoccupied with our neurosis, irregularities, and behavior management, rather than behavior comprehension. The Enneagram, on the other hand, shows us not only the various features of our personality, but illuminates for us the reasons or situations that have caused us to shut down. It shows us the way to eliminate the behaviors or beliefs that are inhibiting our growth, and clears the path for us to have presence of spirit and full participation in our lives.

By showing us ourselves in all of our many aspects, both strong and weak, self-actualizing and self-destructive, the Enneagram gives us the courage and discipline to work through behaviors that we recognize to be toxic. It doesn't show us who we could or should be. It shows us who we are at our best and at our worst. It confirms for us that we already possess the virtues and strengths of our type, and that the only thing preventing us from being our best selves is... well, our worst selves.

Using the Enneagram as a spiritual tool begins with self-observation. Seeing ourselves for who we really are is what puts us on the path toward growth and toward self-understanding. Our knowledge and observations are useless to us if we don't attach some kind of meaning to them. Self-understanding is the process of attaching meaning to the behaviors and traits we see in ourselves. This is what gives us the ability to change behaviors that are limiting and embody behaviors that are self-actualizing. Acting on that change is what ultimately creates self-transformation, and connects us with our full spiritual selves.

The first step in any spiritual path is self-knowledge. All spiritual traditions usually guiding us toward the same fundamental truths, but they offer us different paths to those truths that speak to our various cultures, histories, lifestyles, political views, and, of course, personalities. But since self-awareness is the foundational core of almost any religious or spiritual tradition, the Enneagram can be seamlessly merged to support and enrich any spiritual practice. The Enneagram offers us a bridge toward our highest selves, and that connects us to the Divine, regardless of what you understand the "Divine" to be.

This is what makes the Enneagram different from a religion. The Enneagram offers you no truths; it just shows you the obstacles that are preventing you from accessing the truth. While religions and spiritual traditions offer us an ultimate spiritual goal or universal connection to strive toward, the Enneagram offers us no endgame. The only thing to be revealed is more layers of your own self, and the selves of the people around you. Thus, whatever spiritual truth you are pursuing, the Enneagram can be used to help you get there. The Enneagram connects you to your true Essence, and that connection is what will allow you to open up and become connected to the Divine Essence in others.

The Enneagram is primarily a healing tool. When we find ourselves disconnected, dissatisfied, and chronically at odds with the world around us, the Enneagram shows us the things within us that are blocking us from fully connecting. It won't magically show us how to make our lives easier or how to solve all of our problems, but it does help us to discern what problems are truly external, and what problems are inventions of our own fears. It allows us to see how we are contributing to the situations that make us feel so spiritually crippled and how reconnecting with our true selves can have tangible effects out in the real world.

Just as each of the personality types come with basic fears and root sins, they also come with basic desires and virtues. Understanding your type's virtues and desires are just as important as understanding your type's fears and vices. Often, we have built up an understanding of who our best selves should be, and this prevents us from actualizing the gifts that are already present within us.

Virtues

In Oscar Ichazo's original teachings of the Enneagram, he ascribed to each type a Passion, Virtue, Fixation, and Holy Idea. These are the four cornerstones that essentially form the core of each personality type. Passions and Fixations are negative or self-destructive tendencies, while Virtues and Holy Ideas are positive or self-actualizing tendencies. While working with and understanding all four of these attributes is important for both spiritual and psychological growth, the virtues are the attributes that bring us closest to self-actualization.

Sometimes called Essences, Virtues are the purest manifestation of our type's positive energy (Levine, 1999). When we are fully present and connected, we express our Virtues. Unlike our strengths or positive qualities, Virtues do not tell us how our personality is expressed. Instead, Virtues speak directly to a clear manifestation of our true selves. Our Virtues are the highest expression of self and spiritual connection, what we feel when we are most whole and present.

We experience our Virtues when we achieve a state of complete presence and awareness. In moments when we experience full non-identification with our social identities and personalities, what shines forth from us is Virtue. While it may seem strange that a personality test calls for detachment from your personality, it's not so strange if you take a moment to think about it. Showing you your personality type isn't about placing you in a set category, nor is it meant to give you a set of rules that must be obeyed to achieve spiritual growth. Instead, finding your personality type is about awakening you to the constructions you've placed around your true self. Discovering your personality, paradoxically, is the first step toward letting it go (Riso, 1993). You can't heal or grow beyond something that you don't know exists. This is why the first step is awareness and understanding, and that means working with your personality type to understand who you really are.

In Sufism, the path to self-actualization begins with three illuminations: Illumination of Name (or the cultural/social self), Illumination of Qualities (or personality), and Illumination of Essence (Rogacion, 1991). These "illuminations" outline the spiritual process of self-awareness made possible to us when we work with the Enneagram. The first step is awareness of your social identity. You can't begin to understand your true personality if you don't recognize the false identity that you've built up around yourself. The second step, of course, is understanding your personality. We can only understand our Essence if we first understand our personality, and the attitudes or behaviors that cut us off from that Essence.

When we express our type's Virtue, we have, ironically, experienced a moment when we've been able to fully let go of our personality and simply be as we are. Often it requires intense external stimuli to "wake us up" to our true selves, and open us up in a sudden and brutal way to the Virtue we have within us. Perhaps this "wake up" moment has even happened to you. When we act with grace in a life-threatening crisis or engage instinctively in selfless acts of love, we are fully disconnected from our personalities. In moments like this, we are fully spiritually present, and it is that presence that allows our Virtue to shine through.

As such, the virtues are the opposite of our root sins. Our sins (called "Passions" in Ichazo's original model) are the most negative or destructive expression of our personality. When we express our sins, we experience complete spiritual disengagement. Like the Virtues, our Sins aren't simply negative qualities—they are the inevitable result of too much negative energy and not enough connection or spiritual growth.

As you begin working with the nine types, you will learn your type's Virtue and Sin, and so will begin to understand who you are at your fullest and most beautiful expression of self, as well as recognize who you are at your lowest and most destructive expression of self. The Virtues and Sins aren't states or levels of being to be "attained." We spontaneously express them throughout our lives in moments of pure spiritual bliss and complete spiritual withdrawal. You already have the capacity for your type's Virtue and Sin within you. They are natural expressions of your true self. While the Sin is the natural expression of your true self's ugliness, your Virtue is the natural expression of your true self's beauty. Both live within you, both are part of you, and both are fully accessible to you at any given moment.

What causes us to radiate our Virtues or descend into our Sins has largely to do with how we experience fear. When we give into our fears, we psychologically and spiritually descend, and begin to manifest our Sin more and more strongly and destructively. On the other hand, when we confront, accept, or let go of our fears, the opposite happens. We ascend, and begin to manifest our Virtue more and more strongly and affirmingly. Again, adopting the mindset that your Virtue is something to strive toward or that your Sin is something to actively work against is flawed. You have already attained your Virtue. You have already succumbed to your Sin. The work to be done is with your fears and perceptions. If you can reach a healthy level of presence and self-awareness, then you will make it possible for your Virtue to shine through.

Virtues and Sins work together. Without one, the other is not possible. Our Sins contain within them the key to finding our Virtues, and our Virtues, if we lose presence, can quickly turn into Sins. The goal, therefore, is not to avoid or get rid of Sins. Instead, it's about using our Sins as a key toward better understanding of our true selves. Richard Rohr describes this process in three steps: hold, observe, and trust (Rohr, 1995). When you observe yourself manifesting your root sin, don't recoil from it. Hold onto it. Ask yourself what is blocking you spiritually in that moment. After asking that question, the next step is to observe. Open your eyes to what's really happening. And the final step is trust. Within Sin lies Virtue. Every moment that you engage in your root sin is a moment that could have been engaged in your Virtue. So trust that this moment of destructiveness or negativity is also an expression of your true self, and commit to uncovering the aspects of your personality that are causing this destructive self to appear.

More detail will be given on working with the Virtues in the individual sections for each type. But for now, the Virtues are listed below according to their type number:

Type 1 - Perfection

Type 2 - Freedom or Will

Type 3 - Hope

Type 4 - Universal Belonging

Type 5 - Omniscient Awareness

Type 6 - Faith

Type 7 - Commitment to Work

Type 8 - Truth or Fairness or Justice

Type 9 - Universal Love

Each type follows a unique growth path, a scale along which they move from negative to positive expressions of their personalities. The lower levels of the growth path are more destructive, and engaging in these attitudes and behaviors are often founded on fear and engagement with your type's Sin. The higher levels of the growth path, on the other hand, are more actualizing, and engaging in these attitudes and behaviors are often founded on spiritual connection and expression of your type's virtue. More detail will be given on working through the growth path in the type's individual section, but for now, the growth paths are listed here according to type:

Type 1 - From criticality to judging to serenity

Type 2 - From pride to humility

Type 3 - From self-deceit to honesty

Type 4 - From envy to equanimity

Type 5 - From hoarding to guarding to allowing

Type 6 - From fear to courage

Type 7 - From no limits to restraint

Type 8 - From excess to trusting sufficiency

Type 9 - From being asleep to oneself to righteous action

Practical Points

The Nine Personality Types

So what are the nine personality types? Below is a detailed description of each personality type. Take your time to read through each type and make note of any types that seem to speak to you. You may even be able to discover your type based on these descriptions alone. If not, don't worry, there is a test in Chapter 5 to help you discover your type. But resist the temptation to jump straight to the test. Working with the Enneagram means working with your basic personality type, but it also means working with your type as it relates to all the others. If you don't have at least a basic understanding of each type, you are only seeing a tiny part of the very big picture that is human nature.

Type 1 - The Perfectionist

The primary concern for Ones is doing things right and focusing on what needs correction (Makani, 2010). These people know that nothing is ever perfect—there's always room to improve. Ones place work and personal responsibilities above all else. Duty always comes before pleasure. Ones are sensible, competent, and rational. They have a natural ability to focus on a task and get every single detail right. It's very hard for them to let go of something until it's 100% completed. They seek to avoid mistakes, not only in work or projects, but in personal relationships as well. Things they find to be evil, bad, or corrupted they avoid at all costs, and they have a strict internal critic that helps them to divide the world sharply into categories of right and wrong, good and bad. This binary worldview controls all of their emotions and needs. It's the way that they ensure that they are good people, doing things that are right and fighting against things that are wrong. Ones are rule-followers to the extreme, and have a great respect for authority.

If you are a Type 1, you:
- have awareness of and pay attention to details
- advocate for change and justice

- have difficulty accepting hard realities
- passionately pursue what you believe to be right
- have an idealistic and optimistic worldview
- make rational, balanced choices
- are highly critical of yourself and others
- seek love and approval from those around you
- are deeply motivated by personal values
- chase knowledge and wisdom
- can become obsessive or self-righteous
- defend the rights of others
- are able to connect to and care for your community
- have a tendency to be perfectionistic

Type 2 - The Helper

Twos find it easy to focus on other people's needs, and are always there to provide help and support to whoever is in need of it. They are happy when they receive thanks, and, though they'll never show it, can sometimes feel hurt or underappreciated when their efforts aren't recognized. Paradoxically, though they are highly attuned to the needs of others, it can be very difficult for them to know what they need themselves. They are eager to be liked by others, and will often adapt themselves in order to be the person their loved ones want them to be. This gives them a sense of having many internal selves, and this constant striving to be who others want them to be can make it difficult for them to know who they really are. They love to find exactly what others need, and feel the most secure in relationships where they feel needed. However, they also tend to feel restricted, burned out, or taken advantage of others, especially when they are not praised or rewarded for all of the work that they do.

If you are a Type 2, you:
- have the ability to naturally recognize the needs of others
- easily perceive and understand the needs of others
- are perceived as overbearing at times
- seek acceptance and love from other people
- have a warm, loving, and positive attitude

- attend to the needs of those around you
- have difficulty recognizing and acknowledging your own needs
- repress your own negative emotions
- are persistent and dedicated to the tasks at hand
- fear being unwanted or disliked
- dislike or are easily offended by criticism
- support and encourage those around you
- are driven to get to know other people
- seek and need approval from others

Type 3 - The Achiever

Threes identify with their work or their projects. Ones are incredibly motivated to get the job done and done well, but once their work is done, they are just as happy to turn off their computer and head home promptly at 5. Threes, on the other hand, attach their entire identity to the things that they are involved in. They focus on goals and success, and are hyper-motivated, not only to complete the project, but to gain the rewards, promotions, or other status elevators that come with doing an outstanding job. They are concerned with performance and productivity.

They always know what the next step is, and what they need to do to get there. They care about getting the job done and reaching their goals. For them, there is no distinction between professional and personal life. They take their work very seriously and often take their work home with them. They habitually ignore their feelings and will repress anything that interferes with reaching their goals, including fatigue or personal commitments. They can assume whatever role is needed in order to get the job done. It is difficult for them to take time off, as they often feel insecure or lost without something to work on or strive for. They love To-Do Lists, as they feel good checking off each item as it's completed throughout the day.

If you are a Type 3, you:
- are motivating and encouraging to those around you
- seek validation and acceptance through success
- have difficulty accepting failure from yourself or others
- fear being unworthy and unloved

- are able to understand and connect with others
- are adaptable and high-energy
- lose touch with or avoid your own feelings
- regularly set and accomplish goals
- are charismatic and confident
- focus on your personal development
- are perceived as insensitive or overly confident
- are driven to accomplish and succeed
- think efficiently and practically in the workplace
- focus too heavily on personal image

Type 4 - The Individualist

Fours are concerned about their emotions, and more than any other sign, are constantly soul-searching to find their true selves. They want real and authentic connections with other people, but because they are so introverted and painfully self-conscious, it can be difficult for them to relate to others or relax enough to open up in social situations. Their mood can fluctuate significantly over the course of a day, and they are the most vulnerable type to depression and social anxiety.

Once they are comfortable, however, they are incredibly emotive, and these incredible emotional depths help them to facilitate deep relationship bonds that free up their partners to access their true feelings as well. They are looking for the unique in everything, and they make up most of the ranks in creative fields like literature, music, and the arts.

If you are a Type 4, you:
- are sensitive to and understand the feelings of others
- seek your own identity separate from others
- fixate on what you don't have
- want to leave a lasting impression on the world
- have a general awareness of your own growth areas
- fear having no significance
- have a tendency to focus too much on yourself
- are creative, artistic, and expressive
- are an imaginative, creative, and deep thinker

- seem reserved or withdrawn in large groups
- react strongly and emotionally to hardship
- are able to connect deeply with your own emotions
- are consistently and authentically yourself
- withdraw in times of difficulty

Type 5 - The Observer

Fives love to gather knowledge, and much prefer the company of books or intellectually stimulating podcasts than the company of actual people. They often read a lot and are very knowledgeable on a variety of subjects. They can set aside their emotions very easily, and often prefer not to become too attached to any people, situation, or project. They love to have conversations about things that make sense to them and on topics that peak their interest, but they get very impatient with chit-chat or meaningless small talk. They often have an urgent need to be alone and can find social situations incredibly draining. They want to be independent from others and, like Fours, much prefer to live in their heads than in real life.

If you are a Type 5, you:

- observe the details of your environment
- seek knowledge and deeper understanding
- are perceived as condescending
- prefer spending time by yourself
- constantly learn and pick up new skills
- fear being useless and inadequate
- disconnect from your feelings
- guard yourself and your emotions
- are able to remain calm in a crisis
- are curious about and observant in new environments
- detach or isolate yourself from other people
- think through complex problems
- focus completely on the task at hand
- have difficulty relating to the emotions of others

Type 6 - The Skeptic

Sixes experience a lot of doubt, and are highly prone to anxiety. They are concerned about what can go wrong, and spend a lot of time planning for the worst-case scenario before heading into a new situation. They will carefully analyze each piece of a project to make sure nothing goes wrong, and are very uncomfortable embarking on new undertakings without a firm outline or agenda already in place. They have an ongoing internal dialogue about which decision is best, and it can be very hard for them to take action without guidance or supervision from a more confident person. They can always see a topic from two sides, which makes them fantastic mediators but terrible decision makers. They are looking for people they can trust, and rely strongly on supportive people to feel secure in their relationships. They are very loyal to people, however, and if they decide that you are someone worth protecting, they'll defend you to the death.

If you are a Type 6, you:
- honor commitments to people and plans
- seek security and stability from others
- have a tendency to expect the worst outcome or be pessimistic
- fear losing your support systems
- protect and care for others
- work hard and act responsibly

- fear important or major life decisions
- project your feelings in hard times
- recognize and think about other perspectives
- value loyalty and trust in relationships
- have high levels of self-doubt and insecurity
- make responsible and practical choices
- are able to consider both logic and emotions
- have difficulty controlling anxious thoughts

Type 7 - The Adventurer

Sevens think that life, first and foremost, should be fun. They have many exciting dreams and plans, and are better than almost any other type at making these plans come true. They like to keep appointments open, and feel very uncomfortable making long-term commitments. They are good entrepreneurs in the sense that they often have great ideas for innovative new projects, but have a great deal of difficulty putting in the grunt work it often takes to make these projects succeed. They often have many future scenarios in their head, but unlike Sixes, they are dreaming of the best possible outcome rather than the worst-case situation.

If you are a Type 7, you:
- think quickly and creatively
- prioritize enjoyment and remain optimistic
- have a tendency to grow bored easily
- pursue new opportunities or experiences
- have the ability to see many options or solutions
- fear missing out or being deprived
- are perceived as self-centered or vain
- desire contentment and satisfaction
- are able to easily handle changes in plans
- enjoy being around people
- make impulsive or rash decisions
- justify others' actions to avoid being upset
- can quickly acquire new skills or abilities
- have high levels of energy and optimism
- have difficulty committing to plans in advance

Type 8 - The Leader
Eights love challenges, and they love overcoming them even more. They like to take a leadership role, and find it very difficult to follow orders or

directions from other people. They are fearless when moving towards a goal, and will smash through any obstacles (including people) that get in their way. Others can find them motivating, but they can also come across as pushy, demanding, and even bullying. Eights can be dominating in their drive for leadership, and have a hard time seeing things from other peoples' perspectives. They will fight to the death for what they feel is important, which makes them incredibly powerful allies when they support you and maddeningly difficult to be around when they don't agree with you.

If you are a Type 8, you:
- act quickly and decisively
- stand up for yourself and those around you
- have a tendency to disregard the opinions of others
- are skilled at making hard decisions
- effectively lead others to success
- fear being controlled and losing your autonomy
- have difficulty following rules or orders

- struggle to be vulnerable with yourself and others
- defend and protect other people
- are perceived as argumentative
- take charge when it isn't your place
- are able to express yourself in every situation
- are able to make fair and logical decisions
- are perceived as intimidating

Type 9 - The Peacemaker

Nines find conflict very unpleasant, and will do whatever it takes to avoid it. They find it easy to know how others think and feel, but will often repress their own thoughts or feelings for fear of rocking the boat. Nines like life to be pleasant. Unlike Sevens who want adventure, however, Nines prefer things to be easy, quiet, and undemanding. They like to be comfortable and often postpone changes, making them wonderfully soothing personal companions but terrible procrastinators in the workplace.

If you are a Type 9, you:

- are able to remain calm and adaptable
- avoid conflict with the world around you

- have a tendency to minimize problems
- seek peace and harmony with yourself and others
- support and reassure those around you
- fear loss and rejection
- avoid difficult or upsetting situations
- are accepting and agreeable
- mediate conflict between others
- try to ignore or numb yourself to your problems
- are passive-aggressive rather than addressing conflict
- have the ability to see multiple perspectives
- are open-minded and suspend judgment
- have difficulty facing personal conflict with others

The Triads and the Wings

These nine types can be subdivided into two triads: the Stances and the Centers. The Stances indicate the primary way in which your type relates to the world, and affects how your type projects socially to other people. Types within the same Stance Triad often find it easy to get along with and relate to each other, while different types of

Stances can be difficult for you to interact with at first (or sometimes ever).

The Stances

The Aggressive Stance (3, 7, 8)
These numbers enjoy being in control. They are fully independent and strong-willed, sometimes to a fault. They are constantly looking forward to the future.

For Threes, this manifests as the driving desire to be a "somebody" that is valued by the world. Threes are desperately afraid of being worthless, and so find it difficult to let their precious reputations be ruined or their chances at success compromised by someone on their team not pulling their weight. However, this drive to be successful also makes them incredibly independent, and pushes them to achieve some truly great things.

For Sevens, this manifests as the driving desire to avoid limitations and maintain their freedom. If a

Seven does or doesn't want to do something, it's nearly impossible to change their mind. While this can make them the life of the party, it can also get them (or their friends) into some pretty dangerous and unnecessary situations.

For Eights, this manifests as the driving desire to be strong and dominant. They are natural-born leaders, but if they aren't careful, they can become natural-born bullies as well.

The Dependent Stance (1, 2, 6)

These numbers place a high value on their relationships with others, sometimes even above their own individual needs. They are the personalities most able to remain fully mindful of the present, without becoming tangled in guilts from the past or anxieties about the future.

For Ones, this manifests as the driving desire to be perfect. Ones sharply divide the world into good and evil, right and wrong, and they desperately want to fight on the side of good. This means they'll go above and beyond to protect their ideals, but it also means that if you're doing something that they don't see as "right," they'll do everything they can to show you either the "right" path or condemn you as someone who is corrupted or evil.

For Twos, this manifests as the driving desire to be loved. Twos are extremely empathetic, and will do anything and everything necessary to make the people around them feel warm and cared for. While this usually keeps them focused on the present moment and the people around them, if they do start looking at the past, they can become resentful or feel taken advantage of if their efforts aren't appreciated.

For Sixes, this manifests as the driving desire to be safe and secure. Sixes rely on supportive people around them to make them feel protected, guided, and safe. If Sixes do start looking toward the future, however, it's hard for them to imagine anything but the worst-case scenario, and they need assurance from a more confident loved one that nothing bad is going to happen.

The Withdrawing Stance (4, 5, 9)

These numbers tend to be shy and introverted. They are often looking back to the past for answers to problems in the present.

For Fours, this manifests as the driving desire to find what is missing that would make them complete. Fours are on a continuous soul-quest to find out what makes them valuable and unique, which can make them extremely introverted and reflective. This need to stand out can also make them feel terribly self-conscious around other people, and makes it difficult for them to relate to others.

For Fives, this manifests as the driving desire to gain knowledge and information. Fives much prefer the company of books than people, and are therefore often studying and pondering over that which has already been written, rather than listening to what voices around them are saying right now.

For Nines, this manifests as the driving desire to avoid anger and conflict. Nines will repress any thoughts or feelings that they think someone else might find offensive. Consequently, they are amazing listeners, but can be extraordinarily reticent when it's their turn to open up to others.

The Wings

The Enneagram is a circle, not a list. Each type naturally transforms into the next, much like the colors of the rainbow are not divided by sharp defining lines, but slowly bleed one into the other. As such, this means that every type takes on a bit of the characteristics of the two numbers on either side of it. For example, if you're a Type 4, this means you take on a bit of the characteristics of 5 and 3. The behaviors that you take from your Wing (or Wings) can be entirely positive, entirely negative, or a mix of both (Croft, 2015). Most people have one very strong Wing that exerts a noticeable influence on the core personality. However, some people seem to take a little bit of influence from both Wings, and some people seem almost a pure embodiment of their type, without any discernible influence from their wings at all. That's ok—no combination is right or wrong. It's all about how your type number manifests within you. People never change their basic type numbers, but people do sometimes change their Wings. For example, as a child you may have been a 5w4, but as you have gotten older, you've started to feel and behave more like a 5w6. Sometimes people take on traits from different Wings in different life situations. For example, you might be a Type 3 who works in a creative field, maybe as a writer or an actor, and so your Wing 4 comes out very strongly in your professional life. However, in your personal relationships, you might become very warm, demonstrative, and loving, and become a 3w2. Once you've discovered your basic personality type, the influence of the Wings are often very easy to see, and will become clearer once you start looking for their influences in your daily living.

The Centers

The second (and primary) Triad of the Enneagram is the Centers. This divides the Enneagram star into three overall sections: The Heart Triad, the Head Triad, and the Gut Triad. Each center has to do with the primary way in which each type processes information they get from the outside world, and acts as a kind of filter through which they view all of their relationships with others. Because the Centers are much more subjective and internal, types of the same Center don't necessarily get along easily with or relate to each other. In fact, within each triad, there are three primary expressions of the Center intelligence: over-expression, under-expression, and being out of touch. Paradoxically, the number that is the most out of touch with their Center Intelligence is often the one that is able to use it the most productively, as its influence over them isn't so strong that it's overpowering.

The Heart Center (2, 3, 4)

These three types experience the world primarily through their feelings (Webb, 2013). Relationships and the way that others see them are extremely important to them. They are the most empathetic and intuitive types, and can easily sense what other people are feeling. These types can feel a deep sense of longing or yearning when they aren't in successful relationships.

Twos are the type that over-express their emotions. They are the most emotive type, but sometimes they give too much and don't open themselves up to receive love and support from others.

Fours are the type that under-express their emotions. While they have deep, deep currents of emotion, they are often uncomfortable expressing those feelings directly to other people. They are capable of forging extraordinarily deep connections with people, but if they feel rejected or neglected, their deep emotional depths can quickly turn dark with depression.

Threes are the most out of touch with their emotions. This is both a gift and a curse. On the one hand, Threes are probably the most sociable type, and find it very easy to get along with just about any type of person. However, they sometimes repress their own feelings if they feel like their emotions will get in the way of achieving their goals.

The Head Center (5, 6, 7)

These three types experience the world primarily through their thoughts. They have highly active imaginations, and are able to quickly analyse and solve even the most difficult of problems. These types are most comfortable in their own thoughts, even Sevens and Sixes, which tend to be more social than Fives. These types rely on their own intelligence to get them through life, and can find it difficult to trust or open up to other people.

Fives are the type that over-express their thoughts. Fives and Fours are probably the most comfortable types living in their own heads, but while Fours are looking inward to examine their emotions, Fives are looking inward to examine their thoughts. Fives are constantly studying and learning, and while their ideas may seem wacky to some, many of the world's most innovative minds belong to Fives.

Sevens are the type that under-express their thoughts. Focused primarily on fun, adventure, and excitement, Sevens rarely seem like "brainy" or intellectual people. However, what they often don't share with others is that, underneath their reckless thrill-seeking is a vivid imagination. Sevens are pushed to do bigger and better things because they, too, live in a mental world of their own creation. They're just much better at making that world a reality than Fives are.

Sixes are the type that are most out of touch with their thoughts. This is both a blessing and a curse. Like Fives and Sevens, Sixes have an incredibly fertile imagination, but if they fall prey to anxiety and insecurity, that imagination is spent imagining potential pitfalls and disasters, rather than ruminating over intellectual ideas (Fives) or planning their next big adventure (Sevens).

The Gut Center (8, 9, 1)
These types experience the world primarily through their instincts. These types are all about action, and they often don't waste any time

second-guessing or self-reflecting. They know what they want, and they know how to get it. These types are action-oriented, and are able to make quick decisions with little trouble or anxiety. However, these types are the most prone to social mistakes that, with just one second of forethought, might have been avoided. These types have the quickest tempers. When their anger is righteous, they are champions for the causes of others, but when their anger is destructive, they can be downright cruel.

Eights are the type that over-expresses their instinct. Eights have no social filter whatsoever. They don't doubt for a second that what they think is right, and if others disagree with them, it doesn't matter because those other people are obviously wrong. This bull-headedness makes Eights amazing leaders, courageous defenders of the things they believe in, and staunchly loyal members of any relationship. However, it also makes it very hard for Eights to understand that theirs is not the only right way to view the world, and they can quickly turn into bullies if they lose touch with their empathy.

Ones are the type that under-express their instinct. Ones divide the world along sharp lines of right and wrong, good and evil. However, the world rarely falls neatly into these categories, and much of the criteria for these categories is often subjective and situational. Since Ones are extremely uncomfortable with grey areas, they will go to great lengths to rationalize their support for or condemnation of something, even if it goes against their true beliefs, deep inside.

Nines are the type that are most out of touch with their instincts. This is both a blessing and a curse. Unlike Eights, Nines' instincts actually make them highly attuned to the needs and thoughts of others. However, for fear of offending or rocking the boat, Nines often fail to act, even though they knew almost immediately what the right action would have been.

A Short message from the Author:

Hey, are you enjoying the book? I'd love to hear your thoughts!

Many readers do not know how hard reviews are to come by, and how much they help an author.

I would be incredibly grateful if you could take just 60 seconds to write a brief review on Amazon, even if it's just a few sentences!

>> To leave a review, Please visit
www.**EnneagramReview.SelfRenewal.org**

Thank you for taking the time to share your thoughts! Your review will genuinely make a difference for me and help gain exposure for my work

Discovering Your Personality

Now that you know more about each personality type, you may already know your type, or you may still be unsure. If you're unsure, it's ok. Often learning our type can be uncomfortable at first, and our psychic defenses are sometimes triggered to protect us when we read about our true selves. If you have a strong Wing, you also may be stuck between two options, unsure which one is your basic personality type.

To begin the journey toward discovering your personality, first look at the names of each of the types. These names each speak to a fundamental society role that each type plays, and some people are able to find their type simply from the names alone (you can at least rule a few out this way).

> Type 1 - The Reformer
>
> Type 2 - The Helper
>
> Type 3 - The Achiever
>
> Type 4 - The Individualist
>
> Type 5 - The Investigator
>
> Type 6 - The Loyalist

Type 7 - The Enthusiast

Type 8 - The Leader

Type 9 - The Peacemaker

Look at these nine types, and choose the four that speak to you the most strongly. Now take a look at these list of keywords for the types that you chose:

Type 1 - principled, orderly, perfectionistic, self-righteous

Type 2 - caring, generous, possessive, manipulative

Type 3 - adaptable, ambitious, image-conscious, hostile

Type 4 - intuitive, expressive, self-absorbed, depressive

Type 5 - perceptive, original, detached, eccentric

Type 6 - engaging, committed, defensive, paranoid

Type 7 - enthusiastic, accomplished, uninhibited, manic

Type 8 - self-confident, decisive, dominating, combative

Type 9 - peaceful, reassuring, complacent, neglectful

Of the four types that you chose from the list of names, read the keywords and narrow your list down to two types. For the two types, every single keyword should apply to you, or all but one keyword. If more than two keywords don't seem to fit, eliminate that type.

Now that you've narrowed your possibilities down to two, read through these detailed descriptions of the types in their most actualizing, average, and destructive states. From these descriptions, you should be able to discern which type is your basic personality type.

Type 1 - The Reformer

Ones at their most self-actualizing are able to view the world with true objectivity. They are therefore able to act with both wisdom and conviction. Actualized Ones are reasonable, fair-minded, and conscientious. Their consciences are guided by their principles, rather than controlled by them, and they are able to clearly discern between right and wrong.

Average Ones feel a bit out of balance with their inner guidance. They sometimes cling to their guiding principles, rather than use them as a tool for spiritual or social discernment. They strive for absolute perfection, both in work and in their personal lives, and will accept nothing less.

Ones at their most self-destructive are intolerant and self-righteous. They become obsessed with what they see as evil or corruption in the people around them, and are unable to accept any worldviews that contradict their rigid view of good and bad. They can become extremely cruel to themselves and to others in the name of their ideals, without realizing that they are becoming exactly what it is that they condemn.

Type 2 - The Helper

Twos at their most self-actualizing are able to sustain positive feelings toward others without giving in to resentment or denying their own needs. Actualized Twos are compassionate, generous, loving, and thoughtful. They go out of their way to be of service to people, and genuinely feel good when they are helping others.

Average Twos can become possessive, controlling, or needy when they feel that they're not being appreciated. They want to be loved, but they don't know how to clearly communicate their own emotional needs to their loved ones.

Twos at their most destructive feel a deep sense of rage and resentment, but staunchly deny these feelings to themselves and the people around them. Though they are manipulative and selfish, they will do anything to preserve the image that they are loving and good.

Type 3 - The Achiever
Threes at their most self-actualizing are highly motivated to improve themselves and their relationships. They are able to quickly adapt to any situation without losing their true selves, and are invested in building and maintaining their self-

confidence. They are able to motivate and inspire others through example, and are making a genuine contribution to the world around them.

Average Threes begin to lose touch with their emotions. They are still highly socially attuned, but sometimes they lose their true selves in their attempt to please and be liked by others. They suppress any feelings that get in the way of achieving their goals, and hide any feelings that they think will make others think less of them. In their quest for attention and success, they often suppress their individuality and lose touch with who they really are.

Threes at their most destructive can become hostile and even malicious if they don't receive the praise or attention they think they deserve.

Type 4 - The Individualist
Fours at their most self-actualizing are incredibly intuitive and self-aware. Actualized Fours are personal and revealing and are able to communicate their feelings in a way that helps

others to become more comfortable and aware of their own emotions.

Average Fours become a little too aware of their feelings, especially the negative ones, which makes them incredibly self-conscious. As a result, they often retreat into their imaginations and fantasies.

Fours at their most destructive can become dangerously depressed and feel totally alienated from others. Tormented by self-doubt and self-loathing, they can become suicidal when they are no longer able to deal with reality.

Type 5 - The Investigator

Fives at their most actualized are incredibly perceptive. Actualized Fives are confident in their highly specialized knowledge, and are capable of the most brilliant and innovative solutions to any problem they encounter.

Average Fives lose their ability to bring their thoughts out into the real world, and often retreat into the safety of their imaginations. They become much more comfortable thinking than acting, and can live so much in their own minds that they lose connection with their professional or personal lives.

Fives at their most destructive cause problems, rather than solve them. They become so isolated from reality that they have no ability to discern real from unreal, fact from fiction.

Type 6 - The Loyalist

Sixes at their most self-actualized are able to work methodically and thoroughly through any problem. They are able to foresee potential problems, and are therefore able to act to prevent them. They are loyal, faithful, and unwaveringly committed to their relationships.

Average Sixes retain this foresight, but lose the ability to act. As such, they can become too dependent on an authoritative body or figure to tell them what to do. If they feel like the authority figure can't be trusted, they'll do the opposite and outright rebel.

Sixes at their most destructive become completely overwhelmed by anxieties and insecurities that completely compromise their self-esteem. This often leads to self-destructive behavior that ironically initiates the very problems they fear so deeply.

Type 7 - The Enthusiast

Sevens at their most self-actualized have beautifully rich and active minds. They are able to do whatever they put their minds to with ease. They are enthusiastic and fully engaged, capable of contributing huge amounts of positive energy and talent to every relationship.

Average Sevens become restless, and often move from one activity or topic to another with an inability to commit. The more they move, the less satisfied they feel and the more frantically they search for newer and more exciting experiences. They aim to keep themselves occupied at all times to avoid the anxieties that are lurking in the back of their minds. They constantly feel like they are "missing out," and often complain that what they're doing isn't as good as what they could be doing.

Sevens at their most destructive become totally self-centered and delusional, intent on escaping reality and losing any sense of self-control.

Type 8 - The Leader

Eights at their most self-actualizing have an awe-inspiring vitality and a sharp intuition that often catches the opportunities in situations that other people overlook. They are strong and capable, and use their vast reserves of self-confidence, courage, and leadership skills to inspire others to achieve things they never thought possible.

Average Eights tend to dominate the environment around them. Their need for control can sometimes be a bit aggressive, as they will impulsively assert themselves when they feel like something is happening without their permission or knowledge. They tend to indulge in their instincts, saying and doing whatever they're inspired to do in the moment with no regard for the consequences.

Eights at their most destructive devolve from leaders and motivators into bullies and tyrants. They ruthlessly tear down anything or anyone that doesn't agree with them or stands in the way of achieving their goals or satisfying their needs.

Type 9 - The Peacemaker

Nines at their most self-actualizing are emotionally open and therefore almost psychically empathetic. They are able to see what others are feeling or needing almost immediately and are able to remain calm even in the face of the most trying or dangerous situations. They are receptive, optimistic, and peaceful. These traits radiate out to others and reassure them, creating a sense of harmony and well-being for all.

Average Nines are unable to stay fully present and therefore withdraw a bit from the world around them in order to maintain their inner tranquility.

107

They will often idealize a person or idea that seems to embody for them the "perfect" person, world, or situation, which can lead to a dangerous tendency to live in their daydreams and ignore reality.

Nines at their most destructive become outright fatalistic and neglectful. They cling so much to their fabricated ideals of "perfection" that they lose almost all grasp on reality.

Your Basic Personality Type

At this point, you should have a clear idea of what your basic personality type is. If you're still not sure, or if you want to confirm, there are a number of online tests you can take to verify your feeling. But after reading through the descriptions of the basic personality types, it should be fairly clear to you which one is your basic type. There will be one description that seems to fit like a glove, that feels almost creepily accurate, that gives you the chills because it describes parts of yourself you didn't even realize were there.

That feeling of having the chills is the magic of the Enneagram at work. Now that you've discovered your basic personality type, you'll never look at yourself the same way again. You have a new pair of eyes with which to view yourself and your behavior, but what you do with that new vision is up to you. It must be, as your unique life-path and life situations will be totally unique, even from other people with your same basic personality type.

Discovering your type number often gives you a pretty clear idea of which wing is dominant for you, or if you even have a dominant wing. The influence of the wings should not be underestimated—the same type number with one dominant wing can often behave very differently from someone with the same type number but with a different wing. In fact, different wing types can be so distinct from each other that some have argued that the Enneagram should actually be subdivided into 18 distinct personality types, rather than the base nine.

These are the 18 Enneagram Wing Types:

       1w9 - The Optimist

       1w2 - The Activist

       2w1 - The Companion

       2w3 - The Host

       3w2 - The Enchanter

       3w4 - The Expert

       4w3 - The Enthusiast

       4w5 - The Free Spirit

       5w4 - The Philosopher

       5w6 - The Troubleshooter

       6w5 - The Guardian

       6w7 - The Confidant

       7w6 - The Pathfinder

       7w8 - The Opportunist

       8w7 - The Nonconformist

       8w9 - The Diplomat

       9w8 - The Advisor

       9w1 - The Negotiator

If you're still unsure which wing is dominant for you, take a look at these names. Which one names you most accurately? If you're still stuck between two numbers for your basic personality type, learning the wing subtypes might help you. For example, perhaps you're still not quite sure if you're a 4w5 or a 5w4. Which of the two names describes you better, the Free Spirit or the Philosopher? This can help you determine your basic personality type, and therefore give you insight on how the influence of your wing manifests in your own personality.

However, sometimes the names alone don't quite do each type justice. Below is a basic overview of each of the eighteen wing types to help you better determine which one you are.

1w9 - The Optimist

Basic Fear: Being unethical and corrupt
Basic Desire: To be morally good
You are a 1w9 if you:

- Advocate for peace and justice
- Pursue what you believe is right
- Make rational and objective choices
- Desire love and admiration from others

- Seek awareness and understanding of the world
- Have highly focused attention to details
- Have a tendency to seem detached or impersonal

1w2 - The Activist

Basic Fear: Being immoral and making impure choices

Basic Desire: To be upstanding and humane

You are a 1w2 if you:

- Are aware of the needs of others
- Passionately follow what you believe to be right
- Make principled, ethical choices
- Advocate for social change and justice
- Seek love, affection and time around people
- Defend and stand up for those around you

- Easily grow frustrated with other people

2w1 - The Companion

Basic Fear: Being unwanted by those they love

Basic Desire: Love and acceptance above all else

You are a 2w1 if you:

- Recognize the feelings and needs of others
- Desire love and acceptance
- Serve those around you
- Repress negative emotions and desires
- Fear being unloved or unworthy
- Recognize the needs of others
- Are highly self-critical or insecure in trying times

2w3 - The Host

Basic Fear: Being unwanted or worthless

Basic Desire: To be loved and accepted

113

You are a 2w3 if you:

- Understand and attend to the needs of others
- Seek acceptance and accomplishment
- Enjoy group settings and meeting new people
- Repress your own negative emotions
- Avoid being disliked or undervalued
- Have an optimistic worldview and upbeat attitude
- Have a tendency to be overly competitive or obsessive

3w2 - The Enchanter

Basic Fear: Failing and being unworthy of love

Basic Desire: To be admired and accepted

You are a 3w2 if you:

- Are encouraging and vivacious
- Enjoy setting ambitious goals
- Seek success and accomplishment
- Focus on your social appearance

- Fear being rejected or unworthy of love
- Are dedicated to achieving your goals
- Are heavily focused on social image

3w4 - The Expert

Basic Fear: Failure

Basic Desire: To succeed and feel valued

You are a 3w4 if you:

- Are more constrained and controlled than a "typical" Type 3
- Have a basic fear of being unworthy
- Desire success and affirmation
- Think and process internally
- Focus on your professional development
- Are attentive to specific tasks
- Focus too heavily on professional success

4w3 - The Enthusiast

Basic Fear: That they have no significance in the world

Basic Desire: Uniqueness and personal identity

You are a 4w3 if you:

- Are energetic, distinctive, and driven
- Desire significance and legacy
- Seek uniqueness and individuality
- Fear having no impact on the world
- Engage with those around you
- Are deeply in tune with yourself
- React emotionally in difficult times

4w5 - The Free Spirit

Basic Fear: Having no impact on the world

Basic Desire: Their own personal identity

You are a 4w5 if you:

- Are creative, intellectual, and objective
- Seem reserved and withdrawn from others
- Want to understand the world
- Seek personal impact and identity

- Fear having little knowledge or significance
- Stay true to who you are
- Withdraw from those around you

5w4 - The Philosopher

Basic Fear: Being helpless and incompetent

Basic Desire: To feel helpful and able

You are a 5w4 if you:

- Are guarded or withdrawn from others
- Seek new skills and knowledge
- Curiously explore new environments
- Prefer being by yourself
- Fear being helpless or incapable
- Think creatively and expressively
- Have a tendency to be overly sensitive

5w6 - The Troubleshooter

Basic Fear: Being useless or incapable

Basic Desire: To be competent and useful

You are a 5w6 if you:

- Are a hardworking and analytical problem solver
- Withdraw from others when stressed
- Prefer to spend time thinking alone
- Fear being incapable or incompetent
- Make practical and logical decisions
- Are focused and well-organized
- Struggle to relate to and understand others

6w5 - The Guardian

Basic Fear: Losing their guidance and stability

Basic Desire: Security

You are a 6w5 if you:
- Seek support and guidance
- Are hardworking and intellectual
- Fear losing your stability
- Project your feelings onto others
- Think logically and analytically
- Solve problems practically and efficiently
- Struggle to control negative thinking

118

6w7 - The Confidant

Basic Fear: Losing their support system

Basic Desire: To feel safe and supported

You are a 6w7 if you:

- Love being around people
- Are afraid of losing your security
- Make jokes to defend and project feelings
- Seek support and assistance from others
- Value reliability and trust in relationships
- Dedicate yourself to causes
- Have difficulty reconciling negative emotions

7w6 - The Pathfinder

Basic Fear: Missing out

Basic Desire: To feel fulfilled and happy

You are a 7w6 if you:

- Justify the actions of others to avoid being upset
- Value happiness and optimism

- Fear missing an exciting opportunity
- Seek satisfaction and gratification
- Pursue relationships with others
- Are productive and cooperative
- Are easily affected by others' opinions

7w8 - The Opportunist

Basic Fear: Being deprived

Basic Desire: To be content and satisfied

You are a 7w8 if you:

- Prioritize optimism and gratification
- Seek opportunity and experience
- Are afraid of missing out
- Love the company of others
- Justify negative actions and feelings
- Are high-energy and positive
- Are perceived as impatient and blunt

8w7 - The Nonconformist

Basic Fear: Being controlled by others

Basic Desire: To remain in control of their own lives

You are an 8w7 if you:

- Advocate for the rights of others
- Think practically and creatively
- Are afraid of losing your autonomy
- Dream big and are idealistic
- Struggle to be emotionally honest or vulnerable
- Make logical and fair decisions
- Struggle to remain patient

8w9 - The Diplomat

Basic Fear: Being hurt by others

Basic Desire: To guard themselves against threats and control their own destiny

You are an 8w9 if you:

- Dislike taking orders from other people
- Are more calm and laid back than "typical" Type Eights
- Struggle to openly share emotions
- Fear being controlled by others
- Seek autonomy and independence

- Have the ability to see different perspectives
- Struggle to control your temper

9w8 - The Advisor

Basic Fear: Being separated from the world
Basic Desire: To be internally balanced
You are a 9w8 if you:

- Are afraid of loss and separation
- Avoid personal confrontation and conflict
- Are social and adaptable
- Seek balance and peace in life
- Use routine to ignore your problems
- Encourage and support other people
- Struggle to balance assertiveness and passivity

9w1 - The Negotiator

Basic Fear: Being separated from the rest of the world and losing what matters to them

Basic Desire: Peace, both internally and externally

You are a 9w1 if you:

- Seek routine and moral action
- Fear misfortune and isolation
- Are optimistic and orderly
- Avoid disturbing peace and balance
- Try to numb yourself to your problems
- Can easily see many sides to a situation
- Overlook your own needs

Going Deeper

At this point, you should know two of your four main Enneagram numbers. You know your basic type number, and you know your wing number. You know your basic fear and your basic desire, and you have a better understanding of your basic personality traits, behaviors, and attitudes. But now we are going to delve a bit deeper into the Enneagram, and begin working with the types in more detail.

There are two sections covered in this chapter— the Levels of Development and the Directions of Integration and Disintegration. Each type has strengths and weaknesses, virtues and vices. Each type has the ability to grow and blossom to new spiritual heights, but each type also has the ability to descend further and further into self-destruction. The Levels of Development are like a spiritual map, showing how each type ascends up to the full expression of their virtue and descends into the full expression of their root sin. But before we begin working with this map, it's important to look more generally at each type to understand their basic strengths and weaknesses.

The Levels of Development correspond to your basic personality type. Both wing types will follow the same levels of development. However, I'm listing the strengths and weaknesses below according to wing type to give you a more detailed idea of what your personal strengths and weaknesses may be, so that you have more clarity of vision when you begin working with the Levels of Development.

1w9 - The Optimist

At your best, you:

- Have a highly focused attention to details
- Calmly defend the rights of others
- Care for the community around you
- Consistently abide by personal values
- Have an imaginative yet logical

worldview

At your worst, you:
- Have a tendency to seem detached or impersonal
- Have difficulty tolerating negativity in the world
- Criticize yourself and others
- Become stubborn when challenged

1w2 - The Activist

At your best, you:
- Defend and stand up for those around you
- Are sensitive to the wishes and needs of others
- Are able to serve and improve your community
- Share creative ideas and solutions to problems
- Are willing to make personal sacrifices for other people

At your worst, you:
- Easily grow frustrated with other

people

- Have a tendency to be image-focused or obsessive
- Have the possibility of becoming self-righteous and controlling
- Criticize yourself and others

2w1 - The Companion

At your best, you:

- Recognize the needs of others
- Are aware of your own growth areas
- Focus on and give attention to present tasks
- Offer support and encouragement

At your worst, you:

- Are highly self-critical or insecure in trying times
- Seek praise from others
- Ignore and sacrifice your own personal needs
- Have difficulty facing criticism from other people

2w3 - The Host

At your best, you:

- Have an optimistic worldview and upbeat attitude
- Build deep personal connections
- Are adaptable in stressful situations
- Communicate clearly and effectively
- Have a passion for serving others

At your worst, you:

- Have a tendency to be overly competitive or obsessive
- Don't acknowledge your own needs
- Take criticism personally
- Criticize yourself and others when under pressure

3w2 - The Enchanter

At your best, you:

- Are dedicated to achieving your goals
- Are naturally self-confident and self-aware
- Are able to easily connect with

others
- Care deeply for your community
- Are efficient in the workplace

At your worst, you:
- Are heavily focused on social image
- Struggle to accept failure from others
- Are overly competitive or obsessive
- Have a tendency to be unintentionally manipulative

3w4 - The Expert

At your best, you:
- Are attentive to specific tasks
- Are able to recognize personal growth areas
- Connect with those around you
- Think practically and work efficiently
- Strive to continually improve

At your worst, you:
- Focus too heavily on professional success
- Have a tendency to face self-doubt

in stressful circumstances
- Have difficulty accepting loss or disappointment
- Are perceived as overly confident or moody

4w3 - The Enthusiast

At your best, you:
- Are deeply in tune with yourself
- Understand the feelings and motivations of others
- Think creatively and efficiently
- Are consistently genuine and authentic

At your worst, you:
- React emotionally in difficult times
- Focus too heavily on image
- Face self-doubt and insecurity
- Have a tendency to seek approval from others

4w5 - The Free Spirit

At your best, you:

- Stay true to who you are
- Have deeply-rooted curiosity and passion for knowledge
- Are able to connect deeply with yourself
- Are an objective and creative problem-solver

At your worst, you:
- Withdraw from those around you
- Have difficulty focusing on real-world problems
- Have a tendency to think too much about yourself
- Struggle to follow rules or orders

5w4 - The Philosopher

At your best, you:
- Think and express yourself creatively
- Are able to work well independently
- Observe and understand small details
- Have a deep level of focus and attentiveness

At your worst, you:

- Have a tendency to be oversensitive
- Focus too much on yourself
- Distance yourself from other people
- Struggle to think practically or realistically

5w6 - The Troubleshooter

At your best, you:

- Are focused and well-organized
- Have a passion for learning and growing
- Are able to solve difficult or complex problems
- Remain calm in times of crisis

At your worst, you:

- Struggle to relate to and understand others
- Have a tendency to be private and defensive
- Are perceived as cold or aloof
- Have difficulty taking action when uninspired

6w5 - The Guardian

At your best, you:

- Are able to solve problems practically and efficiently
- Focus on specifics and details
- Are able to work well independently
- Have a passion for pursuing knowledge

At your worst, you:

- Struggle to control negative thinking
- Have a tendency to withdraw from others
- Have difficulty expressing your own emotions
- Are perceived as cold or aloof

6w7 - The Confidant

At your best, you:

- Dedicate yourself to a cause
- Care deeply for other people
- Honor promises and commitments
- Are naturally sociable and spirited

At your worst, you:

- Have difficult reconciling negative emotions
- Struggle to make life decisions
- Have a tendency to doubt yourself and others
- Care too much about material possessions

7w6 - The Pathfinder

At your best, you:

- Are productive and cooperative
- Are sensitive to the feelings of others
- Remain optimistic even in stressful situations
- Think thoroughly and quickly

At your worst, you:

- Are easily affected by the opinions of others
- Doubt yourself and feel anxious
- Have a tendency to become bored in a job or relationship
- Have difficulty focusing or remaining

organized when stressed

7w8 - The Opportunist

At your best, you:

- Are high-energy and positive
- Have natural self-confidence and charisma
- Have the ability to assert yourself
- Remain calm in situations of crisis

At your worst, you:

- Are perceived as impatient and blunt
- Focus too heavily on career
- Have difficulty following through on plans
- Have a tendency to focus on material items

8w7 - The Nonconformist

At your best, you:

- Make logical and fair decisions
- Form connections with others
- Create optimistic and innovative

plans
- Lead others inspirationally and effectively
- Have the ability to share your thoughts and opinions openly

At your worst, you:
- Struggle to remain patient
- Have a tendency to overindulge yourself
- Have difficulty listening to authority figures
- Lack sensitivity to the feelings of others

8w9 - The Diplomat

At your best, you:
- Have the ability to see different perspectives
- Are naturally energetic and confident
- Lead others through support and guidance
- Protect those you care about

- Give attention to the needs of others

At your worst, you:
- Struggle to control your temper
- Have a tendency to be stubborn or rigid
- Dislike rules or orders from authority figures
- Seem overly confident or emotionally detached

9w8 - The Advisor

At your best, you:
- Encourage and support other people
- Have the ability to assert yourself in professional settings
- Adapt to new ideas or circumstances
- Connect with and effectively lead others
- Seek multiple perspectives in a situation

At your worst, you:
- Struggle to balance assertiveness

and passivity
- Have a tendency to avoid difficult situations
- Minimize emotional aspects of problems
- Are perceived as blunt or stubborn

9w1 - The Negotiator

At your best, you:
- Easily see many sides to a situation
- Desire to help and improve the lives of others
- Have a strong work ethic and focus
- Have deeply rooted motivation and purpose
- Have the ability to remain open-minded

At your worst, you:
- Overlook your own needs
- Have a tendency to be overly critical of yourself
- Are perceived as cold or aloof when stressed

- Have difficulty facing conflict head-on

Levels of Development

Now you know what your best and worst traits are, but what you don't know is why you behave the way that you do. The key to understanding the "whys" of your strengths and weaknesses is the Levels of Development.

As you might expect, there are nine levels of development, which can then be divided into three categories: healthy, average, and unhealthy. Levels 1, 2, and 3 are healthy. At these levels, you exhibit your strengths, you express your personality in a self-actualizing way, and at Level 1, you are actually able to let go of the restrictions of your personality in order to begin integrating across the Enneagram. Levels 4, 5, and 6 are Average. At these levels, you are beginning to disintegrate. You are retaining the positive qualities of your type, but you are also highly susceptible to your fears. If you give into those fears, you descend into Levels 7, 8, and 9, the Unhealthy levels. At these levels, you are exhibiting the more destructive aspects of your personality, until you arrive at the lowest level, where your basic fear is realized by your own actions and attitudes.

This chapter will detail a basic outline of the path each of the nine types typically takes through the Levels of Development. Each outline will show you the main actions and attitudes displayed by your type at each level, as well as your type's basic fear at each level, and the subsequent desire that is developed in order to escape that fear. Following the map can show you which fears you need to overcome in order to ascend, and the secondary desires you need to let go of in order to realize your type's basic desire.

Level 1 - Level of Liberation

This is the highest level, and the level at which your type is functioning at its most healthy.

Type 1 - The Wise Realist

At this level, you:

- Let go of your forced goodness, order, and attachment to self-image

- Let go of the belief that you are in a position to judge anything objectively

Behavior: Wise, accepting, noble, pure, kind, realistic

Type 2 - The Disinterested Altruist

At this level, you:

- Let go of forced love and attachment to self-image
- Let go of the belief that you are not allowed to take care of yourself and your own needs

Behavior: Loving unconditionally, altruistic, humble, gracious, joyous, charitable

Type 3 - The Authentic Person

At this level, you:

- Let go of forced value and self-image
- Let go of your dependency on the positive regard of others and your achievements to make you feel valuable

Behavior: Authentic, modest, genuine, charitable, contented

Type 4 - The Inspired Creator

At this level, you:

- Let go of your forced uniqueness and attachment to your self-image
- Let go of the belief that you are missing something that others have

Behavior: Profoundly creative, expressing the personal and universal

Type 5 - The Pioneering Visionary

At this level, you:

- Let go of forced intelligence and attachment to your self-image
- Let go of the belief that you are separate from the environment

Behavior: Participating, knowing, clear-minded, comprehending

Type 6 - The Valiant Hero

At this level, you:

- Let go of forced support outside of yourself and your self-image

- Let go of the belief that you must rely on someone or something outside yourself for security

Behavior: Extremely trustworthy, emotionally open, bonded with others

Type 7 - The Ecstatic Appreciator
At this level, you:

- Let go of forced joy and attachment to your self-image
- Let go of the belief that you require specific objects and experiences to feel fulfilled

Behavior: Can fully appreciate and internalize the depth and meaning of your experiences

Type 8 - The Magnanimous Heart
At this level, you:

- Let go of forced strength and attachment to your self-image
- Let go of the belief that you must always be in control of your environment

Behavior: Compassionate, empowering, gentle

Type 9 - The Self-Possessed Guide

At this level, you:

- Let go of forced peace and attachment to self-image
- Let go of the belief that your participation in the world is unimportant

Behavior: Independent, dynamic, self-aware, exuberant, serene

Level 2 - The Level of Psychological Capacity

This is still a healthy level. At this level you are functioning at full psychological capacity, but are lacking on a spiritual level, as you begin to develop desires and fears.

Type 1 - The Reasonable Person

Basic Desire: To be good, to have integrity, and to be in balance with everything
Basic Fear: Being bad or corrupt

Behavior: Reasonable, conscientious, sensible

Type 2 - The Caring Person

Basic Desire: To be loved

Basic Fear: Being unloved and unwanted

Behavior: Loving, empathetic, caring

Type 3 - The Self-Assured Person

Basic Desire: To feel worthwhile, accepted, and desired

Basic Fear: Being worthless

Behavior: Desirable, adaptable, self-actualizing

Type 4 - The Self-Aware Intuitive

Basic Desire: To have a significant and meaningful identity based on your inner experience

Basic Fear: Having no identity or personal significance

Behavior: Sensitive, introspective, unique

Type 5 - The Perceptive Observer

Basic Desire: To be capable and competent

Basic Fear: Being helpless and incapable

Behavior: Curious, fascinated, interested

Type 6 - The Engaging Friend

Basic Desire: To find security and support
Basic Fear: Having no support and guidance
Behavior: Reliable, engaging, friendly

Type 7 - The Free-Spirited Optimist

Basic Desire: To be happy and satisfied
Basic Fear: Being deprived and trapped in pain
Behavior: Enthusiastic, excitable, spontaneous, adaptable

Type 8 - The Self-Confident Person

Basic Desire: To protect yourself and determine your own course in life
Basic Fear: Being harmed or controlled by others
Behavior: Strong, self-reliant, self-confident

Type 9 - The Receptive Person

Basic Desire: To have inner stability
Basic Fear: Loss of connection
Behavior: Peaceful, humble, gentle, resilient

Level 3 - The Level of Social Value

This is still a healthy level, but at this level we begin to develop secondary desires. We think that if we achieve those secondary desires, then our basic fear won't be realized. But what this actually does is create a new fear that then needs to be combated.

Type 1 - The Principled Teacher

At this level, you:

- Desire to act in accordance with your conscience and reason
- Reinforce and demonstrate your self-image through doing good things

Behavior: Relating to others primarily by being responsible and principled

Type 2 - The Nurturing Helper

At this level, you:

- Desire to do good things for others
- Reinforce and demonstrate your self-image through generosity and service to others

Behavior: Relate to others primarily by being giving and supportive

Type 3 - The Outstanding Person

At this level, you:

- Desire to develop yourself
- Reinforce and demonstrate your self-image through self-development

Behavior: Relate to others primarily through self-improvement and ambition

Type 4 - The Self-Revealing Individual

At this level, you:

- Desire to express your individuality to yourself and others
- Reinforce and demonstrate your self-image through creativity and self-expression

Behavior: Relate to others primarily through creativity and authenticity

Type 5 - The Focused Innovator

At this level, you:

- Desire to master something to gain confidence

- Reinforce and demonstrate your self-image through mastery and innovation

Behavior: Relate to others primarily through innovation and exploration

Type 6 - The Committed Worker

At this level, you:

- Desire to create and sustain support and security systems
- Reinforce and demonstrate your self-image through cooperation and commitment

Behavior: Relate to others primarily through being cooperative and committed

Type 7 - The Accomplished Generalist

At this level, you:

- Desire to do things which will ensure that you have what you need
- Reinforce and demonstrate your self-image through trying new things

Behavior: Relate to others primarily through being prolific, realistic, and versatile

Type 8 - The Constructive Leader

At this level, you:

- Desire to prove your strength through action or leadership
- Reinforce and demonstrate your self-image through leadership and achievement

Behavior: Relate to others primarily through leading, being decisive, and providing

Type 9 - The Supportive Peacemaker

At this level, you:

- Desire to create and maintain peace and harmony in your environment
- Reinforce and demonstrate your self-image through supporting, reconciling, and comforting others

Behavior: Relate to others primarily through supporting and mediating

Level 4 - The Level of Imbalance

This is the first Average level. At this level, you become more attached to your self-image, and therefore are more vulnerable to your fears and insecurities.

Type 1 - The Idealistic Reformer

At this level, you:

- Desire to improve yourself and your world
- Prove your self-image through your social role as the moral teacher

Behavior: Feeling intense personal obligation to do the right thing

Type 2 - The Effusive Friend

At this level, you:

- Desire to be wanted and close to others
- Prove your self-image through your social role as the special friend

Behavior: Believing that you are without needs and always well-intentioned

Type 3 - The Competitive Status Seeker

At this level, you:

- Desire to distinguish yourself from others

- Prove your self-image through your social role as the winner

Behavior: Competing for status and attention

Type 4 - The Imaginative Aesthete
At this level, you:

- Desire to cultivate and prolong selected feelings
- Prove your self-image through your social role as the special one

Behavior: Withdrawing into your imagination to heighten and intensify your feelings

Type 5 - The Studious Expert
At this level, you:

- Desire to feel safer and more confident by retreating into your mind
- Prove your self-image through your social role as the expert

Behavior: Withdrawing into your imagination to heighten and intensify your concepts and mental worlds

Type 6 - The Dutiful Loyalist

At this level, you:

- Desire to reinforce your support systems
- Prove your self-image through your social role as the responsible implementer

Behavior: Becoming dependent on something outside the self for guidance

Type 7 - The Experienced Sophisticate

At this level, you:

- Desire to increase your number of sources of stimulation
- Prove your self-image through your social role as the energizer

Behavior: Feeling that something better is available somewhere else

Type 8 - The Enterprising Adventurer

At this level, you:

- Desire to acquire the resources you need to maintain your position
- Prove your self-image through your social role as the rock

Behavior: Thinking that you are completely self-sufficient

Type 9 - The Accommodating Role Player

At this level, you:

- Desire to avoid conflicts
- Prove your self-image through your social role as the nobody special

Behavior: Withdrawing into your imagination to heighten and intensify your sense of peace and harmony

Level 5 - The Level of Interpersonal Control

At this level you lose a sense of maintaining your self-image for your own sake, and start trying to manipulate and control others. You desperately fear being seen as you are, rather than as who you think you are.

Type 1 - The Orderly Person

At this level, you:

- Insist on being seen as a rational, objective person
- Desire to have consistent order in your inner and outer worlds

Behavior: Manipulating others by correcting them

Type 2 - The Possessive Intimate

At this level, you:

- Insist on being seen as a caring, loving person
- Desire to be needed

Behavior: Manipulating others by making others depend on you

Type 3 - The Image-Oriented Pragmatist

At this level, you:

- Insist on being seen as an outstanding, effective person
- Desire to impress others

Behavior: Manipulating others by charming them

Type 4 - The Self-Absorbed Romantic

At this level, you:

- Insist on being seen as a sensitive, unique person
- Desire to have your identity nurtured and supported by others

Behavior: Manipulating others by being temperamental and hyper-sensitive

Type 5 - The Intense Conceptualizer
At this level, you:

- Insist on being seen as an intelligent, perceptive person
- Desire to shut out intrusions on your space

Behavior: Manipulating others by staying preoccupied with your projects and detached from others

Type 6 - The Ambivalent Pessimist
At this level, you:

- Insist on being seen as a dependable, responsible person
- Desire to resist further commands and commitments

Behavior: Manipulating others by testing their loyalty and trust

Type 7 - The Hyperactive Extrovert
At this level, you:

- Insist on being seen as a happy, enthusiastic person

- Desire to stay constantly excited and stimulated

Behavior: Manipulating others by distracting them and demanding that others meet your needs

Type 8 - The Dominating Power Broker

At this level, you:

- Insist on being seen as a strong, assertive person
- Desire to feel important to yourself and others

Behavior: Manipulating others by dominating them and insisting they obey

Type 9 - The Disengaged Participant

At this level, you:

- Insist on being seen as an easygoing, peaceful person
- Desire to maintain the status quo

Behavior: Manipulating others by blocking out the pressure to change

Level 6 - The Level of Overcompensation

At this level, we begin performing who we want to be, rather than allowing our true selves to shine through. We become extremely anxious about the maintenance of our self-images, and it becomes difficult to make meaningful connections with others.

Type 1 - The Judgmental Perfectionist

At this level, you:

- Desire to criticize others for not meeting your standards
- Undermine others by angrily criticizing them and treating them as if they were defective or bad

Behavior: Perfectionistic, opinionated, black-and-white thinking, impatient, fault-finding

Type 2 - The Self-Important Saint

At this level, you:

- Desire to have your virtue and goodness recognized

- Undermine others by making them feel unworthy of your love and attention

Behavior: Feeling taken for granted and entitled

Type 3 - The Self-Promoting Narcissist

At this level, you:

- Desire to convince yourself and others of the reality of your image
- Undermine others by treating them arrogantly or with contempt

Behavior: Inflating, grandiose, superior

Type 4 - The Self-Indulgent Exception

At this level, you:

- Desire to be absolutely free to be yourself
- Undermining others by treating them as if they had no value or personal significance

Behavior: Decadent, self-pitying, entitled

Type 5 - The Provocative Cynic

At this level, you:

- Desire to scare off anyone who threatens your inner world
- Undermine others by treating them as if they were incompetent or incapable

Behavior: Argumentative, intellectually arrogant, extreme

Type 6 - The Authoritarian Rebel

At this level, you:

- Desire to prove your strength, value, and independence
- Undermine others and their support systems by blaming and scapegoating

Behavior: Stubborn, reckless, blaming

Type 7 - Excessive Materialist

At this level, you:

- Desire instant gratification
- Undermine others by depriving them of things and experiences

Behavior: Flighty, unreliable, feeling trapped

Type 8 - The Confrontational Adversary

At this level, you:

- Desire to have others obey
- Undermine the security and safety of others by threatening to harm or control them

Behavior: Threatening, intimidating, defiant

Type 9 - The Resigned Fatalist

At this level, you:

- Desire to minimize the importance of problems in your world
- Undermine others by making them feel that they have lost connection with you

Behavior: Dismissive, indifferent, unrealistic

Level 7 - The Level of Violation

This is the first Unhealthy level. At this level, we begin to lash out and harm others in order to preserve our self-image and keep our fears at bay.

Type 1 - The Intolerant Person

At this level, you:

- Desire to justify yourself and silence criticism from yourself and others

- Violate your self-image through intolerance of others

Behavior: Inflexible, intolerant, self-righteous, unreasonably harsh with others

Type 2 - The Self-Deceptive Manipulator

At this level, you:

- Desire to maintain the belief that you haven't done anything selfish or wrong
- Violate your self-image through manipulation of others

Behavior: Blaming, guilt-instilling, manipulative, insisting that all of your actions are well-intentioned

Type 3 - The Exploitative Opportunist

At this level, you:

- Desire to preserve the illusion that you are still OK
- Violate your self-image through deception of others

Behavior: Secretive, deceptive, dishonest, willing to sell yourself out to succeed in the short-term

Type 4 - The Alienated Depressive

At this level, you:

- Desire to reject anything or anyone that does not support your emotional demands
- Violate your self-image through your hatred of others

Behavior: Self-pity turns into shame, unable to handle or accept disappointments in life

Type 5 - The Isolated Nihilist

At this level, you:

- Desire to cut off all connections with the world and people
- Violate your self-image through your rejection of others

Behavior: Increasing anxiety from self-isolation, feeling rejected by others

Type 6 - The Overreacting Dependent Person

At this level, you:

- Desire to be rescued by the protection of a strong ally
- Violate your self-image through the defiance of others

Behavior: Leaning heavily on your support systems, taking little initiative, avoiding responsibility

Type 7 - The Impulsive Escapist
At this level, you:

- Desire to avoid your pain and anxiety at any cost
- Violate your self-image through your callousness with others

Behavior: Completely uninhibited, seeking any kind of thrill or stimulation, impulsive

Type 8 - The Ruthless Outlaw
At this level, you:

- Desire to survive and protect yourself at all costs
- Violate your self-image through your ruthless treatment of others

Behavior: Feeling rejected and betrayed by the world, brutal, violent, treacherous

Type 9 - The Denying Doormat
At this level, you:

- Desire to defend the illusion that everything is OK

- Violate your self-image through your neglect of others

Behavior: Allowing yourself to be exploited, resisting dealing with reality or change

Level 8 - The Level of Obsession and Compulsion

At this level, we begin to turn inward and harm ourselves in order to maintain our self-image and keep our fears at bay. At this level, we lose psychological capacity, becoming delusional, compulsive, and breaking with reality.

Type 1

> *Secondary Desire:* To consciously control your unconscious or irrational impulses
> *Secondary Fear:* That you are losing all control of yourself
> *Behavior:* Contradictory, hypocritical, obsessive

Type 2

> *Secondary Desire:* To suppress your negative emotions in order to be perceived as more desirable

Secondary Fear: That serving others is not enough to make others love you

Behavior: Seeking and needing approval from others, becoming overbearing, unable to recognize and acknowledge your own needs

Type 3

Secondary Desire: To do whatever is necessary to support your social image

Secondary Fear: That your falseness and emptiness will be exposed

Behavior: opportunistic, exploitative, duplicitous

Type 4

Secondary Desire: To punish yourself

Secondary Fear: That your situation is hopeless

Behavior: Clinically depressed, self-sabotaging, self-rejecting

Type 5

Secondary Desire: To fend off your terrors

Secondary Fear: That you can no longer defend yourself

Behavior: Delirious, hallucinating, schizoid

Type 6

Secondary Desire: To remove all threats to your security

Secondary Fear: That you will be punished for what you have done

Behavior: Lashing out, fanatical, paranoid

Type 7

Secondary Desire: To avoid all commitments to make space for more opportunities

Secondary Fear: That your negative feelings aren't justified by your situation

Behavior: Unable to commit to plans, easily bored, self-centered and vain

Type 8

Secondary Desire: To be invincible

Secondary Fear: That your resources cannot hold out any longer

Behavior: Terrorizing, rapacious, megalomaniacal

Type 9

Secondary Desire: To block out awareness of anything that could affect you

Secondary Fear: That what has happened cannot be undone

Behavior: Disoriented, shutting down, disassociating

Level 9 - The Level of Pathological Destructiveness

This is the lowest Level of Development. At this point, your destructive behavior has resulted in the full expression of your worst self. Ironically, your behavior in this state, intended to keep your fears at bay, actually makes your basic fear come true.

Type 1

Behavior: Punishing, cruel, condemnatory

Destructive Desire: To rid yourself of the apparent causes of your obsessions and emotional disorders

Basic Fear is Realized: You are corrupted, evil, and unbalanced

Type 2

Behavior: Manipulative, critical, self-righteous

Destructive Desire: To undermine the healthy relationships of those around you

Basic Fear is Realized: You are unwanted and unloved

Type 3

Behavior: Relentless, monstrous, monomaniacal

Destructive Desire: To destroy whatever threatens you or reminds you of what you lack

Basic Fear is Realized: You are rejected as worthless

Type 4

Behavior: Life-denying, self-destructive, despairing

Destructive Desire: To escape your crushingly negative self-consciousness

Basic Fear is Realized: You have lost your identity and personal significance

Type 5

Behavior: Psychotic, deranged, seeking oblivion

Destructive Desire: To leave reality and cease all sensory input

Basic Fear is Realized: You are helpless, useless, and incapable

Type 6

Behavior: Self-destructive, inviting disgrace, self-abasing

Destructive Desire: To escape punishment

Basic Fear is Realized: You are not able to survive on your own

Type 7

Behavior: Out of control, dangerous thrill-seeking, complete lack of self-discipline

Destructive Desire: To seize whatever you can out of life

Basic Fear is Realized: You are in pain and deprived of the good things in life

Type 8

Behavior: Destructive, murderous, sociopathic

Destructive Desire: To destroy everything rather than be forced to submit or surrender

Basic Fear is Realized: You are harmed and controlled by others

Type 9

Behavior: Disappearing, empty, self-abandoning

>*Destructive Desire:* To eliminate your awareness
>
>*Basic Fear is Realized:* You have become lost and separated from yourself and others

Directions of Integration and Disintegration

At this point, you have two of the four numbers you need to fully understand your Enneagram personality. You know your basic type number, and you know your wing number. The last two numbers for you to learn are your stress number and your security number. To learn this, you must follow the directions of integration and disintegration.

The lines of the nine-pointed Enneagram star can be followed in two directions. One direction is the Direction of Integration. Following this direction is the way to find your security number. When your type is feeling secure and fully relaxed, it begins to "integrate" or take on the positive qualities of its security type. The Direction of Integration can be followed in this order: 1-7-5-8-2-4-1 and 9-6-3-9. So if you are a Type 4, for example, when you are feeling secure, you begin to take on the positive qualities of Type 1. If you are a Type 5, your security number is 8. When you are feeling secure, you begin to take on the positive qualities of Type 8.

The Direction of Disintegration traces the nine points of the Enneagram star in the opposite direction. This will tell you your stress number. When your type is feeling threatened, anxious, or stressed, it begins to "disintegrate," or take on the negative qualities of the stress number. The Direction of Disintegration can be followed in this order: 1-4-2-8-5-7-1 and 9-6-3-9. If you are a Type 4, for example, your stress number is 2. When you are feeling anxious or stressed, you begin to take on the negative qualities of Type 2. If you are a Type 9, your stress number is 6. When you are feeling anxious or stressed out, you begin to take on the negative qualities of Type 6.

The Three Instincts

Each person favors a different "instinct," or way that they combat fears and realize their desires. These instincts are different from the stances in the sense that they don't favor any one type. No matter what type you are, you could favor any of the three instincts. Read the descriptions below to determine which instinct you favor. This will give you an indication of how you tend to keep your fears at bay and through what means you will attempt to achieve your desires.

Self-Preservation Instinct

People who favor the self-preservation instinct are focused on enhancing and protecting their personal safety, security, and comfort. Their number one priorities are their physical well-being, financial security, and mental health. No matter your basic type number, if you favor a healthy self-preservation instinct, then you always take care of practical necessities like paying your bills, maintaining your home, and investing in your future. Your type's positive qualities are enhanced by self-sufficiency, discipline, and devotion to self-improvement. If your self-preservation instinct becomes unbalanced, however, then your type's negative qualities will be magnified by a preoccupation with financial and other forms of security and an obsessive relationship with diet and exercise.

Sexual Instinct

People who favor the sexual instinct are focused on creating and maintaining powerful emotional connections through intense and intimate interactions and experiences. Their number one priorities are intimacy, connection, and excitement. No matter your basic type number, if you favor a healthy sexual instinct, then you have deep passions, and aren't afraid to try new things. Your type's positive qualities are enhanced by your desire to create truly intimate connections with those you love and to connect with love itself. People who favor the sexual instinct are more in search of intense emotional connection than physical sexual acts, but they do also tend to seek out deep personal connections with their lovers and partners. If your sexual instinct becomes unbalanced, however, your type's negative qualities will be magnified by a lack of focus, neediness, and promiscuity.

Social Instinct

People who favor the social instinct are focused on creating and maintaining relationships, as well as a sense of personal value, accomplishment, and community. Their number one priorities are interpersonal relationships and group participation. No matter your basic type number, if you favor the social instinct, then you are able to maintain many friendships, feel a strong sense of social responsibility, and work hard to protect the group.

Your type's positive qualities are enhanced by a keen understanding of group dynamics and emotional undercurrents, as well as the ability to adapt to any situation. If your social instinct becomes unbalanced, however, your type's negative qualities will be magnified by an antisocial "us against them" mindset. You might start to test other people to determine who's "with

175

you" and who's "against you." Unhealthy social types need to maintain a sense of belonging at any cost, and so have a tendency to overly conform to a group and stop thinking for themselves.

Sorry to interrupt again, but…

Are you enjoying the Enneagram Self-Discovery? If so, then I'd love to hear your thoughts!

As an independent author with a tiny marketing budget, I rely on readers, like you, to leave a short review on Amazon.

Even if it's just a sentence or two!

So if you've been enjoying the book, please…

Visit www.EnneagramReview.SelfRenewal.org and leave a brief review on Amazon.

I personally read every review, so be sure to leave me a little message.

I'd like to thank you from the bottom of my heart for purchasing this book and making it this far. And now, move on to the next page to the final chapter!

Personal Growth

At this point in the book, you've ingested quite a bit of information. You know your personality and wing type. You know your stress and security type. You know your center intelligence, your stance, and your instinct. You know your basic fear and basic desire. You know your strengths and weaknesses, your virtues and your sins. But what next? How do you put all of these things together to start working toward personal growth?

This chapter will outline a basic guide to help you move through the different layers of the Enneagram. Instead of trying to hold everything in your head at once, you can work through the Enneagram, one aspect at a time, to integrate positive attitudes and habits, identify negative attitudes and habits, and grow slowly but surely to a more whole and well person, both psychologically and spiritually.

The place to begin, of course, is with your basic

type number. Don't even worry about the wings at first. Just work closely with your type. Learn its strengths and weaknesses, motivators and stressors, and observe how those dynamics manifest in your own mind and behaviors. Understand how your type's basic desire affects your decision-making, and how your basic fear can undermine your healthy connections with others. Learn how your type moves through the Levels of Development, and try to determine the level you are at, and what fears you need to confront in order to ascend to the next level.

The Small Things

Thinking about the Levels of Development means looking at your type on a continuum. On one end is your type's "passion" or "sin," and on the other is its virtue. As you move up and down the Levels of Development, you are attempting not to remove your passion, but to transform it into your virtue. Here is a basic table to help you think about the general path of your type's growth from passion to virtue:

Type 1 - Anger and resentment to Serenity

Type 2 - Pride to Humility

Type 3 - Vanity and deceit to Integrity

Type 4 - Envy to Equanimity

Type 5 - Avarice to Generosity

Type 6 - Fear and anxiety to Courage

Type 7 - Gluttony to Sobriety

Type 8 - Lust and intensity to Innocence and surrender

Type 9 - Sloth and indifference to Engagement and action

How To Find Your Wholeness

Once you've become more comfortable working with your type, you can begin to pull all of the pieces of the Enneagram together to find your wholeness. First, begin working with your wing. Understand how its influence affects your behaviors and attitudes, and how it manifests in your own unique expression of those behaviors and attitudes. Begin to learn how your wing enhances your basic type's positive qualities, and magnifies its negative qualities. Determine if you are gaining positive attributes, negative attributes, or both from your wing number.

Once you're comfortable working with the wing, begin to think about your center intelligence. Observe your desires, behaviors, and attitudes through the lens of your center intelligence. Begin to understand the insights that your center enables you to access, as well as the blindspots it creates. Each type, in addition to having a dominant center, also has a repressed center. The list of repressed centers is:

Type 1 - Head
Type 2 - Head
Type 3 - Heart
Type 4 - Gut
Type 5 - Gut
Type 6 - Head
Type 7 - Heart
Type 8 - Heart
Type 9 – Gut

Once you are comfortable working with your type's dominant center, begin working with your type's repressed center. How can you begin to integrate the qualities of the repressed center into your worldview?

From your center, you can then move on to start working with your instinct. Determine which of the instincts you favor, and which of them you repress. Begin to understand how your dominant instinct influences your behaviors and attitudes, and make an effort to integrate your repressed instinct back into your worldview.

The final thing to think about is defense mechanisms. Each type has a basic defense mechanism that they resort to whenever they feel fearful or threatened. The final, and most crucial, step toward wholeness is to be able to recognize the defense mechanism when it rears up in your mind, and take steps to resist its influence. The defense mechanisms for each type are as follows:

> Type 1 - Reaction
> Type 2 - Repression
> Type 3 - Identification
> Type 4 - Introjection
> Type 5 - Isolation
> Type 6 - Projection

Type 7 - Rationalization

Type 8 - Denial

Type 9 - Narcotization

Conclusion

While this book has equipped you with a lot of information, this is only a very basic introduction to the Enneagram. I encourage you to read as much as you can about this amazing spiritual and psychological tool, as this book has only scratched the surface of its complexities. There are a number of resources online and in print that you can find to help you continue to work with your basic type, your wing, and the directions of integration and disintegration. There are also a number of tests you can take online to help you determine your basic personality type, as well as your wing number. If you do want to take an internet test, I encourage you to take more than one for the sake of eliminating the biases that are inevitably hidden within each test.

The blessing and the curse of the Enneagram is that it helps you to see yourself from an objective place. It helps you to identify your psychological tendencies, your emotional needs, and your spiritual path. What you have now is a completely holistic map toward your own personal growth, a strategy that can be applied to any other spiritual, psychological, or physical path you take going forward to continue to enhance your wellness. If you follow other spiritual practices, I encourage you to integrate the Enneagram into your practice, and allow each to enhance the other. The Enneagram is recognized by many doctors and psychologists around the world, and so it can be used as or in therapy to help you work through your psychological growth as well.

The Enneagram can also be married to different personality tests and determiners, and often fits quite neatly into any system of personality determination. From the purely spiritual personality determiners like astrology to psychological tests like the Myers-Briggs, you will probably find that your Enneagram type is not in conflict with the information you receive from these other tests.

Finally, the Enneagram has no overarching religious message, and can therefore be integrated into any major religious or spiritual path. No matter what your religious practices or beliefs may be, you will find that nothing the Enneagram teaches you is in conflict with your religious teachings—at least not ones that are healthy and self-affirming.

There are so many resources available about the Enneagram that you can begin to pursue the Enneagram from any angle that seems most relevant to you. If you are interested in the center, stances, wings, or instincts, there are numerous books and articles written solely about them! Allow yourself to follow what feels right when you're working with the Enneagram. If something is particularly interesting or engaging to you, there's probably a good spiritual reason for it.

It's my sincere hope that the information in this book has awakened you to a tool that will continue to enhance your life for many years to come. I hope that your work with the Enneagram brings you closer to spiritual peace and wholeness, and improves your connections with yourself, the world, and those around you.

If you enjoyed Enneagram Self-Discovery, then you'll love the previous book in this series called **The Fearless Empath Guide**.

Empathy is a unique and beautiful gift. But the constant reception of other people's emotions can cause a roller coaster of stress and anxiety. Learn to strengthen your defenses and replenishing your vital energy to become an empowered empath valued by a world in desperate need of your gift.

To check out this book, visit:
www.Empath.SelfRenewal.org

References

Baron, R., & Wagele, E. So you think you understand me. Harpersanfrancisco, 1994.

Berghoef, K., & Bell, M. The modern Enneagram. 2017.

Calhoun, A. A.. Spiritual rhythms for the Enneagram. 2019.

Cron, I. Road back to you. 2016.

Daniels, D. N., and Price, V. A. The essential Enneagram. Harper San Francisco, 2009.

Heuertz, C. Sacred Enneagram - finding your unique path to spiritual growth.2017.

Makani, H. The Enneagram: Your personal path of growth. 2010.

Palmer, H. The Enneagram in love and work. 1995.

Riso, D. R., & Hudson, R. Personality types. Houghton Mifflin, 1996.

Riso, D. R., & Hudson, R. Understanding the Enneagram. Houghton Mifflin, 2000.

Riso, D. R., & Hudson, R. The wisdom of the Enneagram. 1999.

Rohr, R., & Ebert, A. The Enneagram. Crossroad Publications, 2001.

Stabile, S. The path between us. 2018.

Printed in Great Britain
by Amazon